Praise for *Awakening Gaia*

One of the most exciting things to me is meeting an old soul who has awakened. Fred is one of them. Another even more exciting thing to me is to witness a spiritually enlightened medical doctor.

In this wonderful book he shares his journey of spiritual awakening by following synchronicity. He pays attention to the signs that lead him to access ancient knowledge held in his DNA ... with its roots beginning in Lemuria.

He works with crystals, listens, and allows them to be placed where they lead him on Earth. There is purpose and beauty to this that isn't always obvious to him but he trusts. When the human intention is pure the heart follows. He touches his patients in a special way by doing this. I celebrate his journey and his story in this book. Synchronicity probably brought you to read this amazing book.

— Hawaiian High Priestess Kahuna Kalei'iliahi

D1602416

I loved this book! Fred once again gives a grounded view of the magic that is unfolding as the Earth's crystalline grid becomes reactivated. His eloquent insights remind us that we're all guided by spirit and we are all part of the awakening of Gaia. The timing of this book couldn't be better. You'll find yourself smiling at each of his adventures, trusting that our world is in good hands . . . our hands.

—Jonette Crowley, author of
The Eagle and the Condor & *Soul Body Fusion*

As we move through this pivotal time of collective and planetary rebirth, we experience challenges as well as opportunities unlike ever before. Thus, it becomes increasingly important to discover a bigger picture and actively look for solutions on how we can not only improve our human lives, but also enhance well-being of all species in this multi-dimensional, interconnected world.

While Dr. Fred Grover's superbly-written first book, *Spiritual Genomics,* touched on how changing our DNA through mindfulness improves our health, happiness and well-being, his new book, *Awakening Gaia,* delves into how we can be of service to the well-being and evolution of our beautiful planet, Mother Earth in our unique ways. In *Awakening Gaia*, Dr. Grover illustrates how we can activate ourselves and the earth to full potential by sharing his own fascinating spiritual adventures to sacred sites around the world.

The mystical and shamanic stories from Fred's worldwide adventures contained in this book will surely inspire you and expand your vision. You will see how everything is connected beyond time and space and encourage you to notice the presence of divine synchronicity in your life that will help you open your heart and guide you to discover your life's destiny.

Rooted in both worlds of medicine and shamanism, Fred follows his heart's calling and creates healing for himself, those around him and Gaia. Reading Dr. Grover's new book will bring you to the special place in your heart where you are one with the earth, the universe and all sentient beings. From the expanded space, everything is possible.

I wholeheartedly recommend *Awakening Gaia* to everyone who is looking to experience this elevated awareness with Gaia and walk on the empowered path of creating a world magical, compassionate and beneficial to all beings. Will you join him in this journey?

— Yves Nager is bestselling author of *Hawaiian Rebirth*
and a co-author of the Amazon bestseller,
Inspired by the Passion Test. He also
contributed a chapter to the book
Ilahinoor – Awakening the Divine Human

Awakening Gaia

Awakening Gaia

The Lemurian Crystal Grid

Fred Grover Jr., M.D

Spiritual Genomics Press™
P.O. Box 202562
Denver 80220

Printed in the United States of America

For permission to reproduce parts of this book, speaking engament requests or other questions, please contact the author at fgroverjr@spiritualgenomics.com

Editor: Margaret A. Harrell, https://margaretharrell.com
Cover artwork: Front: Lemurian crystal in author's hand,
photo by the author, Pleiades constellation (iStock 471297753)
Back: Sungate at Tiwanaku (iStock 1169769976)
and Spiral Galaxy (Shutterstock 278931728)
Interior and cover design work by Darlene Swanson, https://van-garde.com

Follow us on the Spiritual Genomics Facebook Page!
Visit us at https://spiritualgenomics.com

Publisher's Cataloging-In-Publication Data
(Prepared by the Donahue Group)

Names: Grover, Fred, 1964- author.
Title: Awakening Gaia : the Lemurian crystal grid /
Fred Grover Jr. M.D.

Description: Denver, Co. : Spiritual Genomics Press, [2019] |
Series: Spiritual genomics | Includes bibliographical references.

Identifiers: ISBN 9781733772228 (pbk) | ISBN 9781733772235 (ebook)

Subjects: LCSH: Grover, Fred, 1964---Religion. | Sacred space--Pacific Area.
| Crystals--Therapeutic use. | Geometry--Religious aspects. |
Earth (Planet)--Religious aspects. | Energy medicine. | Lemuria.

Classification: LCC BL580 .G76 2019 (print) |
LCC BL580 | DDC 203.5--dc23

www.spiritualgenomics.com

Contents

Preface

For thousands of years humans have been aligning temples to the moon, sun, and constellations above. Neolithic circles, Native American kivas, temples, cathedrals, and pyramids demonstrate the importance of these alignments around the world, cross-culturally, as far back as 11,000 BC. Starting in the Stone Age, a few examples include Göbekli Tepe (Turkey), Stonehenge circle (England), the Tiwanaku Pre-Incan temple (Bolivia), Egyptian pyramids, Teotihuacan Aztec pyramids, Maya pyramids (Mexico, Central America), continuing through time at Chaco Canyon kivas (ceremonial structures), the Angkor Wat temple complex (Cambodia), Swayambhunath Buddhist stupa (Nepal), and the Temple Mount (Israel), with its Dome of the Rock, to name just a few. It's likely that other archaeoastronomically aligned sites will be found in the future to even predate Göbekli (11,000 years old). We just need to wait for the ice cap on Antarctica to melt. Perhaps the only benefit of climate change is that we might see something within a few years, given the current rate of glacial ice melt!

Our calendars align with the solstices (where the sun is at the greatest distance from the equator), equinoxes (sun closest to equator) for festivals and the birth dates of prophets. Underfoot, we have further aligned ourselves to the energies of Gaia, Mother Earth, through ley lines, circles, and perhaps even crop circles.

Why on earth do this? Is there scientific evidence to support the benefits of making alignments to the stars or to the perceived energy fields of our planet? Did high priests, shamans, or sages have divine insights that instructed them to align structures and create energetic lines and circles? Are some placements, such as the Nazca Lines (in Peru), designed to communicate with visitors from afar? Did we perhaps have help from intelligent life-forms from our own galaxy or beyond?

Could there be a higher-dimensional intelligence that some of us are tapping into, giving humans and other species these insights? Corals spawn with perfect timing to lunar cycles; humpback whales navigate from Alaska to Hawaii, and bees do their wiggle dance to direct the worker bees to nectar. Appreciating their skills should humble us or at least create a sense of awe in observation of the amazing intelligence of colonial organisms, insects. and animals. Witnessing this innate, instinctual behavior, we must contemplate the capacity we must also carry in our own behavior and decision making. *Have we lost the connection to higher consciousness, while the lower life-forms still have it?* Has the development of our cortex and our thinking brain suppressed it? We are close to a human mission to Mars, but we still can't comprehend our consciousness. Do bees have an ability to connect to a greater cosmic intelligence that guides them to make complex 3-D structures, select queens, and know the time to swarm? Clearly, insects don't have the cortical size to make many of the complex decisions we observe. Looking at the health of the planet and welfare of mankind, it seems most of us have lost this higher intelligence and we need to get it back soon. We are divided as a country and we lack the collective consciousness and capacity to address the threats of climate change, pandemics, and rogue leaders potentially creating a third world war. Is our interest in colonizing Mars a collective consciousness of our need to escape a planet in peril like a beehive that has become stressed? Or is it simply to show prowess over other countries' space programs? China is now planning a base on the dark side of the moon, for reasons yet to be determined.

It's up to us to find ways to mitigate our personal and planetary stressors if we plan to sustain life on Earth. In my first book, *Spiritual Genomics*, I detailed many ways to improve our health and enhance our DNA, such as through sound healing, , connecting to nature, mindfulness, psychedelic medicine, and more. Once we heal and awaken our deeper selves, we can heal others and our planet. As others find their altruistic path in whatever way they are called to do so, there is hope for sustainability and a bright resonate future on earth.

Chapter 1:

Magical Synchronicities and My First Crystal

Topping my list of lifetime questions remains this: "Why have I been called to place crystals around the world? It seems I should be one of the least likely individuals to do something of this nature!

My path has been filled with science and research, beginning in high school, which then intensified as I entered pre-med studies in 1983, followed by deeper science immersions as I completed medical school in 1993 and went on to do my three-year residency in family medicine. I didn't grow up in a household with hippie parents, either. Pretty much a standard American life except for moving around more than most, growing up in Colorado, California, and Texas. I call Colorado home, having lived here the majority of my life, over thirty years.

My father, who just recently retired at eighty, is a world-famous heart surgeon, working eighty or more hours a week, and my mother was a grounded, traditional stay-at-home mom who enjoyed volunteering at church, playing mahjong, participating in garden club, and most importantly keeping my brother and me out of trouble through our teen years. Chakra balancing, sacred geometry and discussing the energetic properties of crystals were never part of our dinnertime discussions.

Perhaps it was traveling internationally with the family as a teen or spending quality time in nature through hiking, backpacking, scuba diving, and other activities that began to change me. While I've had some close calls (nearly died rock climbing and in a car accident), I've not had a near-death experience (NDE). Many who pursued unusual endeavors such as working with crystals have had NDE's or other major traumas, opening them up to explore other realms and dimensions for healing. Did those that had NDE's experience something similar to a psychedelic experience that offered insights of higher dimensions creating awareness around metaphysical, energetic properties of crystals, pyramids, energetic ley lines and other realms?

My best guess is that interest in this field manifested as I became aware of the wonders of the world, and the complexities of the human body that can't be explained. I realized there was much more than science could begin to explain, whether it's the extremely complex interactions of our cells, keeping us functioning as a whole, or the construction of the Great Pyramid. Dissecting the heart, brain, and other organs of the human body in medical school was very enlightening. I marveled at how we differentiated from a tiny ball of cells into an extremely complex walking being that then developed what we call consciousness. I wondered, *Is consciousness simply something my brain formulated as neural tracts, etc., developed? Or is it something we acquire as we connect to the universe? Could the small pineal gland I first saw in anatomy class act as an antenna to connect to the higher dimensions and this thing we call consciousness? Is there coherence of my consciousness with others through a planetary field, or a cosmic field of oneness?*

I began to do more inward work through meditation, opened my mind to all possibilities, and removed bias and filters to even the wildest of ideas or theories of the origins of life. Through this unfiltered meditative practice, synchronistic meetings began to happen and my life flowed in a more natural state. It was OK for me to be critical of a theory, but I'd tell myself to be open to it if there wasn't a way to disprove it. Amplifying my meditative experience through the application of plant medicine and psychedelics, allowed me to explore even further beyond the conscious mind and into a matrix of the universe surrounding us.

I remember beginning to pay attention to synchronicities after reading James Redfield's *Celestine Prophecy*, which seemingly randomly caught my eye at an airport bookstore as I was heading out on a year-long round-the-world journey with my ex-wife in 1996.

After spending the typical seven years of postgraduate work to complete our medical degrees and board certifications, we decided to make this journey in '96 to decompress. Seemed crazy, but we were called to escape and reboot.

Despite carrying $200,000 in combined debt, we borrowed more, rented out our house, and left to travel as minimalists, staying in hostels and carrying what fit in our backpacks. For clothes it was one in the pack and one on our back. We'd purchased round-the-world plane tickets for just four grand each, which only allowed us to go east from one major city to another. We connected the dots to regions with trains, ferries, hopper flights and boats—traveling to twenty-five countries.

I finished the book and honestly didn't think much of the happenchance encounters Redfield mentioned so often. I remained open, however, to the possibility of meaningful "coincidences" (synchronicities).

About four months had passed and I began to observe some strange things, such as—when showing up on the Greek Island of Kos—being invited to the reenactment of the Hippocratic Oath. At a museum, I had run into a physician who was on the island for this rare event, and we happened to arrive the day prior and met him. Just luck, I thought.

A month later, in October, we arrived in Cairo, Egypt, and found a cheap shuttle from the airport into town. Crammed into this poorly air-conditioned van, I struck up a conversation with another American, sitting next to me. I soon learned he was studying cartography and was also on a round-the-world trip himself. He hopped off in a different part of town and we headed further into a region near the Nile to wander around, looking for a nice hotel in our price range. Two days later I ran into him at the Saqqara step pyramid and, thinking nothing of it, said a quick hello. After an amazing month, seeing the pyramids and making a cruise down the Nile to Luxor, we flew off to Southeast Asia, landing at the foot of the Himalayas in Kathmandu, Nepal. We were here to explore the mountains, the culture, and do volunteer work. After returning from rural medical-volunteer work in the Langtang mountain-range area, I felt inclined to try out a meditation class offered by a Buddhist monk not far from our lodging in the Thamel area. I walked into a small group of six and found him sitting there, waiting for class. OK, now this is a little weird. I didn't know he was going to Nepal and sure had not expected to see him randomly in a meditation class. We caught up briefly after class, and I wished him safe travels.

Three months pass and we decide to go on a multinight sea kayaking trip in the scenic Abel Tasman National Park on the South Island of New Zealand. The second day, about twelve miles out, we paddled past some seals basking in the sun on a small island. After taking a few pics of the lounging seals with my compact camera loaded with Kodachrome 64, I looked down at my waterproof map bungeed to the deck and saw an inviting trail. "How about we paddle over to this trailhead and make a short hike for a swim under this waterfall?" "Sure," she said.

Sea Kayaking at Abel Tasman National Park with his Theresa (photo by a friendly fellow kayaker)

Our tandem kayak beached and tied off, we began our hike. About halfway along a narrow, single-track trail, we passed a couple returning to the beach. About five steps later we all turned around and stared. "OMG, is that you, David?"

"Fred, what on earth are you doing following me around the world?"

"Ha! I wish I could say I was, but this is just another chance encounter with you! What is going on? This is insane to run into you on a random, remote trail two days into a kayak trip!" We all shook our heads in disbelief as he headed back to his kayak and I headed off to the waterfall. I had an unusual feeling that day, and a message that clearly informed me not everything in the universe is random. While I have not seen him again—I've lost his contact information—I remain confident our paths will cross one day! Perhaps he'll find me through this book. What does synchronicity have to do with crystals? As we continue this journey in the upcoming chapters, you'll see the clarity emerge.

Fast forward to 2005. I'd been practicing medicine for about eight years and distinctly remember one patient out of thousands; in addition to having some basic medical issues, she raved about the healing powers of crystals. I remember it photographically. I can picture her sitting there and me thinking: *Wow, this gal is crazy. Is she delusional? What DSM-5 diagnostic criteria does "crystal-healing thoughts" fall into?* (That's the *Diagnostic and Statistical Manual of Mental Disorder*s, fifth edition, published by the American Psychiatric Association.) As I listened to her talk coherently, calmly—noting she was clearly oriented—I decided I was prematurely assessing her, as often happens to physicians in a rushed insurance-based practice. Most would have coded her as potentially schizophrenic and referred her to psychiatry without listening to her stories, which were not about curing cancer with crystals, but rather of simply feeling healthier, in love with life. Having heard her out, I told her to keep working with crystals. Thinking nothing of it. I continued my work in the grind of seeing twenty or more patients daily as a family doc.

About a year later while hiking up in the colorful fall aspens near Breckenridge, I decided to visit a rock shop on Main Street, called "Nature's Own"— loaded with fossils, gems, and crystals from around the world. Kids love the place, especially since they can hold million-year-old shark teeth, ammonites, and ancient stones. This day, I wandered over to a glass case that displayed some of the more rare and beautiful gems. Amongst them, a simple walnut-shaped clear crystal caught my eye, seemingly out of place, as it was only twenty bucks and lacked the almost psychedelic colors of the surrounding gems. Walnut-sized, it had a central concavity that gave it a more unique shape.

The author's very first Lemurian crystal, which helped spark it all (photo by the author)

I sat there, staring at it in curiosity, and decided it needed to go home with me. The owner wrapped it in some newspaper, enclosing a sheet of paper detailing where it came from and its basic properties. The small, index-card-sized paper read: "Lemurian seed crystal, from Brazil, is a silicon dioxide mineral displaying ladder-like groves crossing the bodies with a clear interior."

"Cool info. Thanks," I said. According to Robert Simmons and

Naisha Ahsian, coauthors of *The Book of Stones: Who They Are and What They Teach*, Lemurian seed crystals connect to the divine feminine, unification of the soul, access to knowledge, and the wisdom of ancient Lemuria. They affect primarily the crown (seventh) and soul star (eighth) chakra. Spiritually explained on the healingcrystals.com site:

> Metaphysical Legend states that there was once an advanced ancient civilization called Lemuria, similar to Atlantis but more spiritually developed and peaceful. As . . . their time on Earth was coming to an end, the Lemurians programmed these crystals to teach their messages of oneness and healing—messages that would be revealed when the energy on Earth was ready to receive them. The Lemurians then planted (or "seeded") the Lemurian Crystals, encoded with their ancient knowledge and wisdom, to be found centuries later by us.
>
> The legend continues to state that Lemurian Seed Crystals are planted in a grid pattern over the surface of the Earth and beyond, to other stars and dimensions. When you connect to a Lemurian Crystal and the energy it contains, you are also connecting to this grid of associated energies from the Earth, the stars, and beyond.

Arriving back home in Denver, I placed this intriguing crystal on my bedside table, not knowing what to do with it. It sat there for weeks, hanging out, when at some point I decided I would place it on my forehead between my eyebrows and begin meditating with it and later that year began experimenting placing larger Lemurian crystals on my 3rd and 4th chakras.

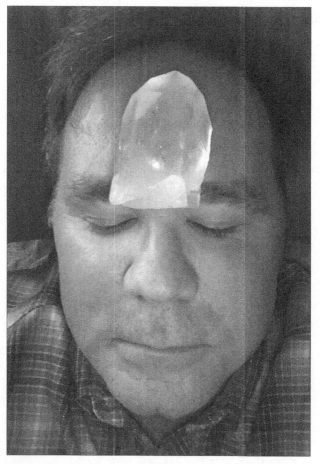

Author with Lemurian Crystal on Third Eye (photo by Keaton Grover)

For some reason, I was drawn to placing it on the Third Eye region as I lay down, eyes closed, on my back before going to sleep. I'd meditate, listening to mantra music, for an hour most nights, visualizing myself connecting to the cosmos, feeling drawn to Pleiades often. Several nights passed. Nothing happened—other than me being startled as the crystal clunked onto the wood floor when I dozed off and rotated that way.

Continuing this routine, with my wife commenting that it was a bit weird of me to do this, I surprisingly had something begin to happen one night. I was a week into my meditation when I began to feel a tingling where the crystal contacted my Third Eye. As I made very slight adjustments, I could feel the energy intensify or decrease as I honed in on the exact location. Suddenly I felt a surge of energy flow from this area, shooting down my spine to my feet. It was similar to an orgasmic flow, but rather than ascending, the crystal was sparking a descending flow. The more intense pulses made my legs lightly contract and honestly freaked me out a bit, initially thinking I was having some kind of complex partial seizure! This repeated most nights, with three to six pulses of energy. Some nights were particularly intense. The flow seemed random, not correlated with solstices and other important astronomical or astrological events. The only relationship I've found is that the location can impact the intensity of energy flow. Doing this in sacred areas or nature often magnifies it, as does working with shamanic plant medicine. I'll go into this more later.

My experiment with this one simple crystal continued for at least a year, at which point I decided to seek out more Lemurian crystals at the rock-and-gem show held annually in my hometown of Denver. My son, eight years old, joined me and has continued to look forward to the show every year. Like me, he relishes in the diversity of stones, minerals, crystals, and fossils. Denver's show is the second largest, with Tucson holding the largest in the world. It was a bit overwhelming. Hundreds of stands were set up to sell everything from Jurassic-aged fossils to large geodes, meteorites, and crystals six feet tall or more that cost over $50,000. That day, we went searching for small- and larger-sized Lemurians. After a couple hours we found a vendor from Brazil who had primarily large crystals, most over four feet tall. But on the tables he had beautiful flats of them, ranging in size from 1 inch to 12 inches. I decided to purchase a flat of about fifty small ones, and then several larger ones.

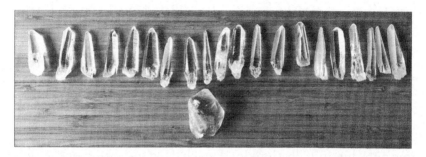

Lemurian Seed Crystals, selected from a flat of crystals later used in an upcoming destination (photo by the author)

Not sure what I was going to do with them, I brought them home to see what might manifest. This type of crystal has small lines perpendicular to the length of the crystal, and for this reason many call them record keepers. The lines, they believe, have data embedded, much like a USB flash drive. However, the amount they can store far exceeds that of any flash drive. In fact, the "Superman memory crystal" can store up to 360 terabytes of 5-D data, safe for billions of years. Elon Musk's Tesla Roadster sent into outer space has one of these crystal discs loaded with data.[1]

Home with the new crystals, I experimented, lining them up on my chakras. I found that a double-terminated (two-pointed) crystal resonated perfectly with my heart; others with the other chakras. I continued to meditate, lying down, placing the largest, a six-inch crystal, between my legs at my root chakra and using medium-sized ones for all the others except the smaller one at my Third Eye. I did this at least once a week; other days, I simply did the heart chakra and Third Eye placements. Additional crystals seemed to further amplify and flow the energy from root to crown, and vice-versa.

I became curious about studying shamanism. And though I never spoke about it, one week three patients on different days said I should study it; two gave me advice where to go! I was blown away that no one had ever said a thing before, and then within one week three recommended it. Of course, I knew this was more than coincidence, so in 2010 I booked a long weekend course with a gal teaching Michael Harner's shamanic methodology in Colorado Springs and was then called to pursue Peruvian shamanism shortly afterwards.

I proceeded to dip my foot in the pool of shamanism cautiously, afraid it might be too dangerous, exceeding some kind of spiritual boundary for my soul. Recognizing the potential for dark energies in shamanism, just as they can be present in any spiritual or religious devotion, I set the intention to stay only in the light and avoid any darkness. I would not abandon Christianity, but would augment my spirituality by flowing into this expansive state.

A few months later I was studying with the "Heart of the Healer," Pachakuti Mesa Tradition group founded by don Oscar Miro-Quesada. We met most months for three days of meditation and teaching. This particular form of shamanism is practiced more in the Andes of Peru and may use the Chavin culture plant medicine cactus Huachuma with mescaline psychoactivity, rather than ayahuasca of the Shipibo shamans in the rainforest regions of the amazon. Both plants possess powerful healing and psychedelic properties. Huachuma was called San Pedro by the Spanish, since they could see Saint Peter in visions, after drinking the tea.

The author's mesa, used for meditative purposes following principles of the Pachakuti Mesa Tradition (photo by the author)

Doing meditations in circle with twelve others, I found myself connecting deeply to Mother Earth and the stars above. We used a "mesa" to place items representative of the four winds, and articles that were meaningful to us from a spiritual standpoint. My mesa consists of a Buddha, cross, stones, crystals, and sacred geometric items lying on an Amazonian Shapibo Indian cloth from Peru. I don't consider it an altar, but a meditative tool that can help me connect to the cosmos, the Christ or Buddha consciousness, Mother Earth, and more. Unlike an altar, it has a noticeably open feel, allowing the light energies of a higher-dimensional universe to flow through it and into the individual. Lasting just over a year, the training helped me do much inward work that is not possible in a traditional church or organized religious setting. I felt myself connecting to the god within me and everyone, expanding into a compassionate state of oneness with all.

After this, naturally I wanted to travel and experience the energies and plant medines of Peru, so in 2011 I booked a summer trip! My intention was to delve into the highlights of the country with the family for ten days, then to spend another week on my own going deeper as I hiked the Inca Trail. They had no interest in hiking this challenging trail, so they flew back home after seeing Machu Picchu at the end of the tour, and I returned to the trailhead near the town of Ollantaytambo to begin my five-day journey back to it on foot.

Chapter 2:

The Inca Trail and Birth of the Lemurian Crystal Grid

The initial ten days in Peru were fascinating as we toured Cusco, the Sacred Valley, and Machu Picchu, but I was now craving a deeper, more spiritual connection to the Andes Mountains and the energies amongst them, hoping to find it as I hiked the Inca Trail.

I joined a small guided trek with four Canadians and our support team of two guides and a few porters. It was sweet to have someone carrying my gear, leaving me simply with my daypack loaded with water, camera gear, basic trail supplies, and a handful of crystals that seemed to want to join me. I had no plans for the crystals—my intention being to flow into what they might be called to do. The first couple days of hiking were intense, as we headed to the top of Dead Woman's Pass at an elevation of 13,828 feet. The family of four from Vancouver in our group had been training for the trip, so I had to push myself to keep up. At this pace, we arrived at each camp prior to the other groups on the trail, which gave us our pick of where to set up tents. Luckily, they allowed me to slow them down a bit as I stopped to take in views and photograph the misty mountains, and ruins.

Near the summit of Dead Woman's Pass we halted, and our guide placed a few coca leaves on what appeared to be a rock cairn (man-made pile of stacked stones). Reaching into my pack, I pulled out my Ziploc® full of them and placed three in between some stones.

Coca leaf, source: https://commons.wikimedia.org/wiki/File:Folha_de_coca.jpg

We drew three more out to make an intention and then with a powerful exhale blew them from our fingertips off the mountain ridge. For the prevention of altitude sickness, I'd brought a big bag to chew on and was happy to have some extras for ceremonial purposes. The leaves are used by Peruvians to make a stimulating tea or an offering to the gods, and historically aided, in the hands of skilled shamans, in predicting future events.

I asked if the pile of rocks was perhaps an apacheta (similar to a cairn but larger). "Yes, that's why we're making an offering." "Thanks. I sensed that." I'd learned about apachetas in my shamanism fellowship. They are used to honor Mother Earth (Pachamama), or often a nearby *apu* (mountain spirit), and play a role in weaving a web of energy amongst other apachetas in Peru and elsewhere, balancing the planet. They may follow a linear ley line (natural energy line on the planet) or can serve to connect the energies between sacred sites. According to shamans, there are many energetic lines of apachetas connecting to Cusco from Machu Picchu and other important sacred sites around Peru. Many ancient cultures, including the ancient Puebloans from Chaco Canyon just eight hours from my home, in New Mexico, created lines of energies.

The author's personal Apacheta in his backyard

As I stood looking at this lonely apacheta, I sensed its energy flowing in various directions, just as the dendrite of a neuron— being not simply a link from point A to point B—sends impulses to different regions of our human brain. Pondering these insights, I began to wonder if shamans positioned apachetas for Planet Earth with a healing intent that's similar to the way an acupuncturist places needles along a meridian line to relieve back pain or improve blood flow or lymphatic flow or amplify Qi (life force energy). Suddenly, I had the insight to grab one of my crystals and place my first crystal. Holding the crystal to my heart, my Third Eye, I breathed some energy into it and placed it between the rocks as deep as I could in the apacheta.

Fred at the Sun Gate of Machu Picchu in 2011 (photo by a fellow hiker)

Wow, what am I doing this for? It seemed so natural yet surreal, with an element of déjà vu. The group had taken off down the trail. I had to jog to catch up. A few miles further, we came to another apacheta, where I placed some coca leaves and a crystal. I continued to do this along the way till on the last day, we woke early to climb up to the Intipunku, or Sun Gate. The Sun Gate, at an elevation of 8,924 feet, was the original entrance to this sacred sanctuary. On this clear morning we observed a beautiful sunrise, followed by the light illuminating the lush green grass and magical Machu Picchu below. Feeling the sacredness of this gate, I decided to hide a crystal between two large rocks next to the gate. Blessing the crystal and the gate, I rejoined the group to hike down to the temples.

The energies of the site were much more palpable than what I'd experienced on my first visit. Was there some kind of attenuation of my energy body that occurred as I hiked the trail, just as the ancient Incas had done? Could the journey be just as important as the end point? The majority of modern tourists I observed likely came to check it off their list, but failed to tap into the deeper essence. Selfies were not mainstream back in 2011, and apps had been available only a few years. The selfie app had just been released with the iPhone 4, and I hadn't made the upgrade yet. Today, thanks to selfies and social media, Machu Picchu has become a popular share, raising it to one of the modern-day seven wonders, along with the Maya site of Chichen Itza discussed later. Pulling out my trusty SLR and keeping my primal iPhone in the pack, I framed the sacred site, with Wayna Picchu and other mountains at various angles—clearly not immune to its photographic appeal.

However, as I composed my photos I began to notice features and alignments that I'm not sure would have popped out at me otherwise. For instance, how the hillside terraces leading up to the prominent Intihuatana at the summit create a *step pyramid-like* geometry.

Machu Picchu at an angle displaying step-pyramid-like terracing (photo by the author)

The Intihuatana, at the top of about seventy steps, "is a wonder of the ancient technology, . . . a kind of clock to measure when was the time to celebrate the winter solstice, called by the Incas

INTI Raymi, one of the most important celebrations and rituals of the entire Empire"[2]; it was carved out of granite. Because one of the main Inca gods was the sun (*inti*, in the Quechua language), "it was important for priests to observe the sun and understand it. So, they had an astronomic clock or calendar that indicated some significant celestial periods for them. This clock was called *intihuatana*."[3]

Intihuatana, aka "Hitching post of the Sun" (photo by the author)

Under their entry, Wikipedia explains that *huata-* is simply Spanish for *wata-*, "the verb root 'to tie, hitch (up).'" And "the Quechua *-na* suffix derives [from] nouns for tools or places. Hence *inti watana* is literally an instrument or place to 'tie up the sun,'" or, in English, The Hitching Post of the Sun.

The alignments of Machu Pichu to the Huayna Picchu mountain, with the sacred site nestled in the saddle between them, seemed so perfect, sighted through my camera.

Machu Picchu with Huayna Picchu in background (photo by the author)

Having captured the essence on a memory card, I sat down on a rock away from the crowds and meditated. (This was before they instituted the regulations of a strict one-way travel circular route at the site.) We had a few hours to explore on our own before meeting up around lunch, so I relaxed and tapped into the energies. I could feel a light tingling coming up my tailbone, ascending my spine, and then creating a similar tingle at my crown and Third Eye. Despite guards blowing the occasional whistle at a tourist going out of bounds, I redirected my focus to the field of energy flowing through me. It seemed to come in pulses similar to how the crystals had done as I meditated to them. At some point, I felt complete with my meditation, and whatever was being uploaded or downloaded into my energy body. I decided to wander back into the temple regions, called to place the remainder of my crystals there in existing wall cracks, with the intention of honoring the site and reconnecting it to the apachetas along the trail.

Ceremonial hut near Pisac, where I attended my first ayahuasca ceremony (photo by the author)

Saying goodbye to my amazing guide and the family I trekked with, I was met by a shaman's assistant in the town of Aguas Calientes. To finish my deep immersion into this area, I had planned an ayahuasca journey. While I'd have preferred to travel to the rainforest, I was lucky to find a retreat center that had a Shipibo shaman (from the rainforest) who performed small sacred ceremonies near Pisac. I began my diet and started to drink a special mineral water that night, prior to taking the train back to Ollantaytambo to participate in a ceremony not far from where I started the Inca Trail. This was not something I decided to do on a whim, but had been called to do for over a year.

After another day of a special diet and offerings by the shaman, we began ceremony in a circular hut with an open roof and fire-dancing flames centrally.

Ayahuasca plant image (Shutterstock)

I go into great depth about this journey in my initial book, *Spiritual Genomics*. As I let go and let "Grandmother Aya" do her work, I began to see the energy lines of Machu Picchu. It was as if I were hovering over it and watched the emergence of the most vibrant colors, ranging from iridescent blues to fluorescent greens, climbing up the citadel from the base to the high point, much like one would see lights illuminating a radio tower. It would light up the base of the pyramid, then the next level, as it seemed to high-light the energy flow going to the Intihuatana. Perhaps what I was seeing on my ayahuasca journey was the energy of Pachamama (Mother Earth) connecting to the cosmos through the base of Machu Picchu and flowing through the apex at the Intihuatana. So I didn't see it as tying up the sun, but as acting more like a transmitter and conduit connecting the energies bidirectionally between this sacred place on Earth and the infinite cosmos above.

I had noted how the terraces—as I mentioned in photographing them earlier—created a pyramid-like structure from the land-scape, but had not expected to see them shown to me as an aerial view in psychedelic colors during a shamanic journey. Light then radiated from the high point of the site. Sacred geometric shapes were visible in the sky and surrounding landscape. I could see now why the Incan priests called the rectangular stone at the summit a "hitching post" of the sun, as I could see the most intense energy being emitted from this point. I could see the light of apachetas connecting to the site from this high point too. Had my crystals somehow impacted the strength of the connection to this sacred temple embraced between two mountains? While some might see this as something akin to an LSD trip, I feel an insight was being shown to me while spirit-traveling to a higher dimension through the Third Eye-opening effect of N,N-Dimethyltryptamine (aka DMT, "the spirit molecule").

The journey continued for another couple hours with many other amazing visuals coming in. When I returned from my spirit travel to Machu Picchu downvalley, I looked down and could see my light body below, with meridian lines and chakras being shown to me.

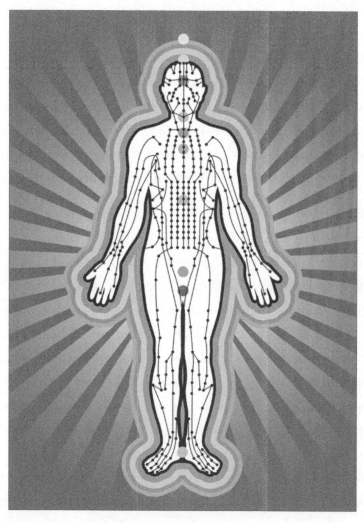

Acupuncture and meridian lines (iStock)

This confirmed what Chinese and Ayurvedic medicine discovered thousands of years ago. After this, I had incredible visions of my DNA being scanned for imperfections, followed by me physically purging energetic garbage that needed to be cleared from current and past lives. As I purged into the bucket handed to me, I didn't simply see the liquid, but saw instead a spiraling black hole sucking away these negative energies from my body and sending them to another realm. While this was not a near-death experience, this plant medicine opened me up in a way that seemed close to NDEs I've heard about. Not as exotic as Dr. Eben Alexander's visions in *Proof of Heaven*, but trending in that direction. The following morning with the shaman I integrated what I'd seen. He sincerely felt my visions were accurate representations of energies in the area, myself, and beyond. I packed my bags and hopped in the van to head back on the windy road, ascending terraced hills to Cusco. Looking out at the Urubamba River and making the multiple switchbacks out of the Sacred Valley and into Cusco felt surreal. Catching my flight the next morning, I gazed out the window over the rugged snow-capped mountains to my right, contemplating all I had experienced. Again, the Inca Trail portion of my trip seemed so dreamlike, beyond a 3-D experience. Arriving back in Denver, I felt shifted into a more balanced state, which created a sensation of more passion, happiness, and lightness than when I'd left. A much more complex shift than simply feeling relaxed after a beach vacation. Tapping into the energies of the Andes and placing the crystals to honor it and the sacred temples felt like mission accomplished. Was this really the finish line, or did I have more work to do? Time would tell.

Chapter 3:

Palenque, the Emerald Jewel of the Maya

Arriving back home, I found it difficult to share with family and friends the details of what I'd felt energetically on Machu Picchu and the multidimensional out-of-body (OBE) travel visualized during the succeeding shamanic journey. I shared what I felt was reasonable and comprehensible to them at that time, avoiding content that might prompt them to book an appointment for me for a mental-health evaluation! If only I could have replayed the visions in a holographic manner over the dining-room table while narrating impressions of what I'd seen, I would have been confident, sharing it all.

I often think of visions, or "altered states" that our biblical prophets have had, and wonder if they too were working with plant medicine such as the Greek kykeon or otherwise able to go into a transcendental state via prayer or meditation to gain insights and then return to a "normal" 3-D conscious state to share with others.

So what is the difference between these various levels of consciousness? According to Tanaaz Chubb, a contributing writer to the *Huffington Post* and co-creator of the website Forever Conscious with Dr. Wei Chao, 3-D is how we view things in their physical state: how we view ourselves as an individual under an ego identity. In 4-D, we begin to resonate with the idea that we are all connected and there is more to life than what we see in 3-D; mindfulness-based activities and a healthy lifestyle become a priority. When you begin to connect to the field of oneness, that's 5-D: more heart-centered, compassionate, and connected to Gaia and the cosmos.

I feel it within the norm for individuals to have visions and insights when doing meditative work, shamanic plant-medicine work, and prayer that may induce brainwave states of high theta and gamma activity. These brainwave states have been noted in highly experienced meditators, such as Buddhist monks, allowing them to flow readily into 5-D states.

Returning to my practice that next day, I felt a bit of reality jolt, as a large stack of lab reports had piled up for review on my desk. Several forms needed to be signed, and patients to be called back. Not to mention bills to pay, and all the other things that come along with running a solo primary-care practice.

Lots of deep breaths, and a steady flow of clearing off the desk (between patients and at the end of day) allowed me to make it through my first week back. Seems like there's always punishment for me taking a vacation. Regardless of the struggle, something peculiar was happening as I was seeing patients. I was listening more, sensing a greater intuition of what was going on with their conditions and overall health. There was more depth to analyzing patients beyond their history and exam, and documenting it in the computer. I found that my diagnostic skills were best when I simply looked into their eyes and followed their story. As the famous Canadian physician Sir William Osler said, "Use your five senses. Learn to see, learn to hear, learn to feel, learn to smell, and know that by practice alone you can become expert." Agreeing with him, I would simply add that we also need to add our sixth sense: intuition.

Months passed quickly, with my busy medical practice, family life, and weekend fun spent hiking or skiing depending on the seasons. I continued my meditation, but began to do more of it on a "sound lounger" in my basement.

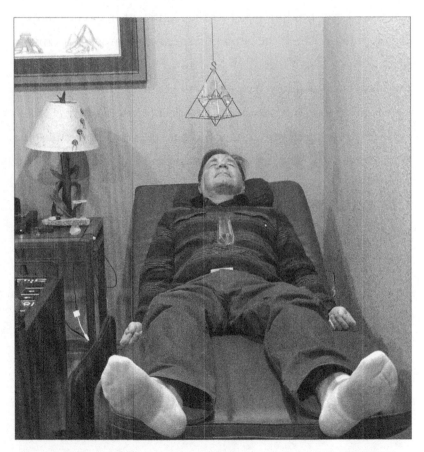

The author in his meditative room alchemizing energies, using a sound lounger resonating mantra music, a pulsed magnetic field therapy, and sacred geometry. Aka humorously called: Captain's chair for interstellar travel! (photo by Keaton Grover)

This amazing tool allowed me to listen to my favorite mantra music in a reclined position while music was resonated from small donut-shaped speakers through the wood and memory foam into my body. I'd listen to Deva Premal, Krishna Das, Snatam Kaur,Ajeet, Mirabai Ceiba, Porangui and others—finding that the sound entrained me into deeper meditative states. Listening to frequency-based music or chanting by artists like Jonathan Goldman and soundtracks of binaural beats worked amazingly well too. Binaural beats (typically listened to over headphones) provide a different frequency to each ear, helping to entrain the brain into specific brainwave patterns for meditation. I began to experiment more with aligning crystals on my body and would even hold sacred geometric objects designed by Gregory Hoag (Metaforms). This effect of resonating my whole body while listening through headphones created a powerful sonic entrainment, relaxing me deeply, taking me into the profoundest states. Last, but not least, I added a pulsed magnetic field therapy via a powered mat pulsing at Schuman frequency on the sound lounger. This modality alchemized with the sound and crystals to further open and balance my chakras.

One evening while I was meditating in this way in my basement space, Pleiadian energies came intensely into my field, sensed especially through the crystal on my Third Eye. I relaxed into what was coming in and received a message that I needed to "reawaken" the energies of a Maya sacred site known as "Palenque," with crystals. I thought to myself: *No, I thought this was a one-and-done thing. Why are you asking me to go there?* I tried to dismiss the message, but Maya pyramids in the rainforest kept reappearing in my deep meditations. I decided to read up on this Maya site, which was the home of Pakal (603–683 AD), considered the most spiritual of all Mayan kings. Interestingly, I found a book titled *Chariots of the Gods* by Erich von Däniken in which the author details his interpretation of Pakal's sarcophagus lid as depicting him riding on a spaceship. The more mainstream archeological opinion is that Pikal is climbing up the traditional Maya World Tree towards paradise and resurrection.

Replica of Pical's sarcophagus lid by local unknown artist, purchased by author on Palenque grounds. A rocket or the sacred world tree?

I'm open to either possibility, but after seeing so many Maya sites and other alien-like imagery, I'd vote for the more controversial and bold theory of Erich von Däniken.

There seemed to be so many mysteries about this less-traveled-to Maya site that I decided to book a trip in November 2012. I had already been to Chichén Itzá, Tulum, and Tikal, and other sites, but never to Palenque, which is more difficult to access. Looking it up on Google Maps, I discovered it is near the State of Chiapas, Mexico, incidentally an area in which until his capture in February 2018 the boss of Las Zetas, one of the largest drug cartels, initiated major operations.

Hmm, traveling to this region on my own will be getting a strong thumbs down from the family. Luckily, after many discussions the family gave into my free-spirit intentions, and I booked my flight from Denver via Houston to the town of Villahermosa. I had uploaded the most recent maps to my old dash-mount Garmin™ GPS so that I could rent a car and hopefully make the three-hour drive without any wrong turns or an ambush from one of the cartel gangsters looking to prey on a lost gringo.

Looking out from my portside (left) plane window about halfway between Houston and Villahermosa, I gazed far into the stars, peering into the southwest and up high. It was a crystal-clear view at 30,000 feet. To my surprise as I gazed into the starry night, the Pleiades constellation was in the center of my vision. *OMG*, I thought. *This is the constellation that gave me the message to come here, and now I'm seeing it brighter than ever, staring back at me 444 light years away.* I sat there in disbelief, with tears running down my cheeks momentarily, and stayed focused on it for another thirty minutes. Within an hour, around 9 p.m., our plane landed and I took a cab to a nearby hotel. I wasn't crazy enough to make the three-hour drive to Palenque ruins that night!

The next morning I returned to the airport to rent a car and begin the road trip through rural Chiapas.

I'm a calm guy, but I was pretty darn nervous the morning I sat down in the car and mounted the GPS on the window. Deep breaths… I plugged the address in and sent a prayer to have my angels and spirit guides protect me safely to and from Palenque on this treacherous drive. Amazingly, navigation went very smoothly; the rough roads were tolerable. I made it to a lodge just a few miles from the archeological site before sunset and settled in. I'd packed a good thirty Lemurian crystals and placed them in a nice pouch to carry with me the next day. Having smudged them with aromatic smoke of Palo Santo, I was excited to see where they might be called to land. Palo Santo is a wood used for clearing (aka smudging) negative energies in a person, place, or thing. A member of the citrus family, also called "Holy Wood" by the Spanish, it grows wild in Central and South America. In North America, sage is more popular for this purpose.

Sage and Palo Santo alongside the back of my shaman drum (photo by the author)

I was restless during my first night, feeling the surrounding energies, and was awoken by the eerie sound of howler monkeys nearby in the rainforest. Luckily I'd heard them in the rainforests of Costa Rica a few times; otherwise, it would have freaked me out.

The next morning I grabbed breakfast in the thatched outdoor restaurant. A few Germans were eating near me, but we seemed to be the only ones in the resort during this off season in November.

Driving up to Palenque took a few minutes, and as I pulled into the park entrance I noticed several guides approaching. Since things were slow, they were hopeful of being hired. I bought my entrance ticket, and they continued to swarm me. But I decided I wanted to do the tour alone after the annoying encounter. My plan was to become familiar with the site on my first day, and on the second day return to place crystals where I felt called to do so. I walked into the forest and up the steps, handing my ticket to the entrance guard. After another twenty feet, an elderly man seemed to appear from the forest to my left and extended his hand. I looked into his brown eyes to sense his inner-being and shook his hand feeling his energy. He smiled, saying gently, "My name is Victor, and I will be your guide." I almost laughed. Really? This guy just appears out of nowhere in the forest to announce he's my guide. I took a breath and tapped more into the moment and his deeper essence. Yes, he is my guide, spirit told me. After this pause, I smiled back and said to him, "Yes, Victor, I would like for you to guide me."

Palenque guide, Victor Hernandez (photo by the author)

We walked down the trail to a limestone courtyard that opened up to the Temple XII (Moon) and XIII (whose lavish decoration earned them the title Funeray Corridor). With its rabbit-skull relief, Temple XII is also called Temple of the Skull. Adjacent to these smaller pyramids is the Temple of the Inscriptions.[4] As I stood there, looking at these pyramids, I felt a rush of energy through my spine similar to what I'd felt at Machu Picchu. The infamous K'inich Janaab Pakal I lies entombed in Temple of the Inscriptions. I thought to myself as we walked: *I'm ready; bring it on, baby.*

Temple of the Inscriptions (photo by the author)

Right away, we seated ourselves on a bench in front and, looking me in the eyes, he said, "Fred, I am here to tell you the real story of Palenque. I started working here in the early 1960s as a laborer, excavating with the archeologists. None of the other guides have been here more than ten years. They don't know the secrets." Big flow of energy again as I try to ground myself while listening. *Wow, I don't believe I'm hearing this. How on earth did this guy find me, or how did I synchronistically find him, dodging the other guides?*

"You see this pyramid in front of you? Deep inside it at the base we found a small Buddha statue. You won't see it in the museum or documented in the books, because the archeologists can't explain it. It's an enigma." I am going to show you many examples of art on this site that demonstrates how the Mayas were in communication with Asia and Egypt and shared knowledge, art, and architecture."

Walking with him, I felt a sense of sacredness underfoot with every step I took. Either I had been here before or the site was energetically connecting to me. He led me to the famous tomb Temple of the Inscriptions, where he spoke of the mysterious sarcophagus lid and the spiritual life of Pakal. K'inich Janaab Pakal I, or Pakal the Great, also called 8 Ahau and Sun Shield; his long rule over Palenque lasted from 615 till he died, sixty-eight years later, in 683. This was "the fourth-longest verified regnal period of any sovereign monarch in history, the longest in world history for more than a millennium, and still the longest in the history of the Americas."[5] He created some of the finest Maya art and architecture in his capitol city, including the palace with its iconic tower. In an article, Christopher Minster tells us he "was buried in jade finery including a beautiful death mask, and placed over Pakal's tomb was a massive sarcophagus stone, laboriously carved with an image of Pakal himself . . . Pakal's sarcophagus and its stone top are among the great all-time finds of archeology.[6]

Even more awaited. Next, the guide led me to the palace region, an unexpected area for the Mayans. As the Ancient History Encyclopedia explains, "Uniquely for Maya cities, at Palenque a royal residence and not a temple is the central focus of the city. The place, likely first begun by Pakal and with major additions such as the tower c. 721 CE, is one of the most complex architectural structures at any Maya site." [7]

Author with the Palace of Palenque in background (photo by a friendly tourist)

Here I saw the classic **corbelled** arches found at many Mayan sites. In the center of the palace stands what appears to be a unique lookout tower, but more likely served another purpose. Near the tower Victor pointed out a carved relief with legs positioned in classic Egyptian pose, and another relief with someone in lotus pose. Around the corner he showed me a relief very similar to a Chinese dragon head. Illustrating his theory of early interaction between the Mayas, Asia, and Egypt, he pointed out numerous other cross-cultural examples as we toured the extensive site. Running beneath the pyramid were tunnels built by the Mayas to channel the water under the pyramid and the main palace. Was this done intentionally to infuse energy into the area, or simply as practical drainage of a spring above it? Similarly, the Pyramid of Kukulkan, at the Chichén Itzá archeological site, which we will get to in Chapter 6, is built over a narrow stretch of an aquifer that opens to the north cenote (natural pit or sinkhole) and to another cenote, south of it. There appears to be an intentional alignment with naturally flowing water for energetic or spiritual purposes.

Hiking around this large archeological site for another couple hours, I viewed the grandiose ballcourt and several other pyramids. The ballcourt here is much smaller than the ballcourt at Chichén Itzá, but still impressive. Every time I walk through one of these, I still ponder the theory that the winners were decapitated after the game! By midafternoon, he'd finished the tour and wished me well. I wished him well too and went over to Temple of the Foliated Cross to meditate.

Temple of the Cross complex (photo by the author)

I had so much to process after this amazing gift of him showing up, providing these mysterious insights. Archeologists have yet to explain this and many other riddles about the Maya. Recent laser radar (LiDAR/light detection and ranging) has revealed that the Maya empire was two to three times the size of what was earlier estimated by archeologists. Their history will continue to be edited as new discoveries are made. (See the *National Geographic* story "Exclusive: Laser Scans Reveal Maya 'Megalopolis' below Guatemalan Jungle.")[8]

Returning to the lodge in the evening, I slept much better, despite the howler monkeys' spooky barking from the canopy of the nearby trees. The rainforest heat and humidity had worn me out.

The symphony of chirping birds awoke me early, and I headed back to the site alone, with my satchel of crystals. My goal was to flow with this sacred site energetically and see where they might be called to land. Away from the crowds, I meditated for a good hour on the back of a pyramid to drop into the energies. I could sense the priests holding a timeless ceremony in one of the subterranean spaces below me. After feeling connected to the site, I wandered in a somewhat random fashion, dancing with the energies, and placed them gently in deep open cracks of pyramids and the palace region.

While there are strict rules against damaging any archeological site or taking a stone, I have not seen anything in regard to leaving a small crystal. If a crystal is ever found, I'm hopeful they will simply leave it there. Unfortunately, many seem to think it is OK to litter trash on these sites, which seems disrespectful to say the least.

After another meditation, I felt the energies of the site increasing and had the desire to place some in the stream flowing through it. This seemed perfect, as when water flows over a crystal it energizes and structures the water to a higher resonant field for the temples and land below. The famous Japanese researcher Masaru Emoto demonstrated how—by flowing naturally in a stream, or by having crystals added, or even when love and compassion are sent to it—water can restructure to a more beautiful geometry. As crazy as this sounds, he's been able to document it in frozen-water samples in his books, cf., *The Secret Life of Water*. Intuitively sensing this, and finding it to be further reinforced by Emoto's research, enlightened me to the importance of making placements in streams, lakes, and oceans.

Left side: Polluted water from the Fujiwara Dam. Right side: Geometric impact of Buddhist monk chanting "Heart Sutra" to the polluted water. Photos by Masaru Emoto from *Messages from Water*, as discussed by Jonathan Goldman.

Hiking below the Palenque pyramids, I discovered beautiful waterfalls and placed more crystals in the clear azure pools surrounded by lush emerald vegetation.

As I drove back to the lodge I was questioning what on earth I was doing and for what purpose! But I shrugged off my concerns, realizing I was back in the 3-D world, driving a car—dodging potholes and navigating this windy, narrow road partially canopied by the lush rainforest trees.

Waterfalls of Palenque (photo by the author)

That night as I did my Third Eye crystal meditation in my room, I sent more love and prayers to the pyramids to reconnect them to the cosmic energies. Similar to how I felt in Peru, a deeper, more intimate connection to the land, the people, and the sacred energies of the site emerged into my auric field and seemed to expand to the higher dimensions surrounding me. I could feel the Maya connections to other cultures around the world, including ancient Atlantean roots. Beyond this, I sensed their connections with those outside our solar system. Perhaps Pakal's tomb, interpreted as a world tree or spaceship, actually represents portals to higher dimensions, or even other worlds. Crazy as these insights and my work here seemed, it felt right. I returned home, once again feeling like my work was complete.

Raven (photo by the author)

Chapter 4:

Chaco Canyon, the Call of the Raven

Several months passed, and my busy days in the office often wore me out mentally and emotionally. Following dinner I'd reboot myself relaxing on my sound lounger with a pulsed magnetic field pad under me to clear my mind and help stave off the burn-out that so many of my colleagues have succumbed to. As with most mantra meditations resonating through the sound lounger, I'd feel a state of bliss and energy flow. Occasionally when I meditated for hours more deeply, I would get what I call "downloads." These downloads typically come as an insight, or sometimes as a visual, or orgasmic-like pulse of energy when I am deep into it. Don't worry, I didn't make a mess of the sound lounger. Ha! Sometimes they'd come in my sleep; other times I had to work hard for them meditatively.

I could see how it takes the mental discipline and isolation of a Buddhist monk to achieve enlightenment, nirvana, the Tibetan Buddhist "Rainbow Body," etc., since getting just a small download was a lot of work for me in most cases. While I'd love to achieve or even briefly experience some of those states, my chances are limited unless I go live in a monastery or ashram for decades.

One evening I was admiring my beautiful cedar Native American flute, which looked lonely on my bookcase. A "high spirit's" flute, it has embedded turquoise between the finger holes. I've jazzed it up with some carved-bone Kokopelli charms, hanging off leather strands. Kokopelli is the Native American deity of Hopi and other tribes in the Southwest, who represents the spirit of music and fertility.

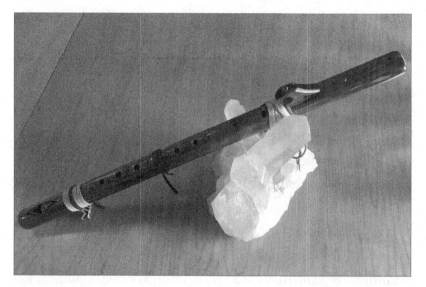

The author's flute (photo by the author)

Having not played it for a while, I blew off the dust. Honestly, I'm not really worthy of owning this beautiful flute, since after ten years I still haven't mastered this six-hole instrument. As I began to play, even with a few basic notes I felt enticed to continue. While I can't play like Carlos Nakai, a well-known Navajo/Ute professional flutist with several amazing albums, I could sense his love for this instrument and his lineage connected to it. So pure, natural, and simple. Playing such a Zen-like instrument alone or amongst canyon walls of the desert Southwest is heaven on earth. As I've played my Native American flute amongst the canyon walls of Sedona and other areas of the Southwest, I felt like its tones breathed life and Qi into these sandstone chambers, reawakening the ancient spirits. The canyon walls seem to respond in an eerie way, echoing and expanding the tone—enchanting those present, physical and nonphysical.

Playing it again that week in my family room and over the weekend, I felt a calling to return to Chaco Canyon. Fall was around the corner, so timing was perfect. I blocked off a long weekend, packed my car camping gear, and headed off for the eight-hour drive. I had selected another large group of Lemurian crystals, just in case I was called again to place them. I saged them, blessed them, even placing them on an apacheta in my backyard the preceding day to energize them before making the solo drive down.

Arriving on a Thursday around three, I was able to find a nice campsite where large boulders on either side provided protection from the wind and some shade as well. Even had a picnic table, firepit, and some wood the last camper had left. *Wow, I'm glamping!* I set up my tent quickly and went down to get in an evening hike before sunset. With only a couple hours to hike, I decided to go up on the Alta Trail, but felt pressured to complete the long loop walking fast enough to avoid getting a ticket for being inside the park after-hours, beyond sunset.

Passing by the massive Pueblo Bonito complex, I parked my old Subaru; shouldering my daypack, I headed up a narrow trail to the top of the mesa. Once on top, I could see most of the ruins of Chaco in the valley below. The almost birds-eye view from the mesa gives perspective on the massive number of kivas found at this ancient Puebloan (Anasazi) site. Kivas are subterranean circular chambers that were used for religious ritual, political, and even family space by the ancestral Puebloans.

Kivas at Chaco (photo by the author)

Walking alone on this mesa trail, I sensed an eerie presence of ancient Chacoans hiking with me, perhaps guiding me to places where I should leave crystals. This unusual field of energy supporting me felt like it was coming from an ancient multidimension field.

Admiring the scale of this site and the kivas below one more time, I headed away from the mesa edge and towards the north on the three-mile loop.

The massive complex of Pueblo Bonito with its forty kivas, taken from the top of the mesa (photo by the author)

Coming to a weathered, half-buried kiva near Pueblo Alta, I burned sage to purify the area, sprinkled tobacco, and then placed a crystal in each of the four directions close to the interior kiva walls. Using my trusty compass, I oriented them perfectly.

Lemurian crystals for Chaco (photo by the author)

I then spiraled the energy up and down with my rattle and played a short melody on my flute to further reactivate this sacred site. I took my time, picking up my pace as I scampered across the sandstone mesa. Scrambling though two fins of sandstone, I eventually emerged back down on flatland. Ravens circled overhead as the sun created an orange glow on the sandstone mesa, highlighting the contours and fissures with growing shadows. The wind was light, and the temperature crispy that fall evening. Sunset was approaching and I was about a mile from the parking lot.

I was trekking along at a good pace, when a large raven suddenly landed in front of me on the trail and squawked loudly at me. I stopped briefly, then continued walking, thinking he would just fly away. Instead, he just flew a good twenty yards down the trail, turned around, and squawked at me again. He repeated this maneuver three times—at which point I stopped and stared at him. Telepathically I was trying to tell him, "Buddy, I am in a hurry and I'm going to get a ticket from Ranger Rick if ya don't let me through." He kept up with a nonstop *craw, craw, craw*, and I said to him, "OK, what is it?" He then hopped off to the left of the trail another twenty yards, and seemed to beckon me to follow. So, I did.

He quickly took me to the rim of the mesa, where interestingly enough, the large D-shaped formation of Pueblo Bonito was just a couple hundred feet below us.

Pueblo Bonito with its D-shape visualized from mesa (photo by the author)

Relieved not to spy a ranger next to my car, I could see it below to the west. Taking some deep breaths and feeling into the situation, I relaxed more with the crow on the rim. He sat there patiently, just looking around and cawing at me. I almost cawed back at him. Looking down again, I realized we were perfectly aligned with the center of Pueblo Bonito. If one were to place a giant arrow in the string of the straight line of the D shape, the arrow nock on the bowstring would align with our location. Wow, I thought. Perhaps this intelligent raven has led me here to place a crystal. He's probably been watching me the whole time. Looking for a place to wedge a crystal into permanence, I noted that everything was solid sandstone except for a small lip that curved under just before the cliff edge. Kind of dangerous, but maybe I could tuck one under this natural indentation. I reached into my pouch and pulled out a beautiful four-inch Lemurian seed crystal. The twilight gave it a beautiful gold glow. I could feel its radiant energy tingling the center of my right palm.

Perfect, I thought. I dug out some sand from under the lip with my fingertip and decided to widen it a bit so I could tuck this baby in deep for eternity. I felt something solid while doing this and was able to remove it with a little jiggling. Must be a small piece of sandstone, I figured. Pulling it out, I was amazed to see a quartz crystal of similar size and shape to the one I was getting ready to place! I cleaned it off—stunned at what I was seeing. How did this similar crystal get here? There are no crystals any-where on the mesa, just sandstone and limestone.

As I looked at my crystal and the other one I'd just discovered, I felt a sense of timelessness, a calmness, and a recognition that this was not happenchance. The raven had led me there for a reason. The reassuring insight that came in was basically this: *Fred, you are not crazy, placing crystals around the world; you're being guided by spirit to do this deep work for Gaia.* Trying my best to take it all in from my conscious 3-D world and beyond, I contemplated the extremely unlikely probability that one could find an almost identical crystal in this location. Recognizing the huge odds against it, I accepted the insight with gratitude to the raven and whatever mysterious forces were surrounding me on the mesa.

I looked at the shiny black feathers of the raven glistening from the setting sun and then gazed into his eyes. He had stayed with me during this timeless moment. Thanking him from my heart, I broke into tears, sitting there, crying some, and trying to figure out what to do. Seconds later the answer was clear. Pair them up and place them back in this sacred location. Perhaps you will return to place a third crystal in another life. Doing this, I packed them in firmly with surrounding sandstone and blessed the event, the raven, and the location. By now the sun had set, the raven had flown off, and I was walking back in the dusk to my car. At this point, I didn't care if I was ticketed. Arriving in near darkness, I found no ticket, and no ranger there to reprimand me for my late stay. I hopped in and drove about one hundred yards to the bridge, crossing a desert wash. As I looked to the east, I gazed at a huge cottonwood tree on the bank. To my amazement I saw—silhouetted by the grey-dusk sky—at least one hundred ravens perched on the expansive branches. I felt an obligation to honor them, since I'd been shown the sacred place to leave a crystal by one of them.

I parked on the bridge, turned off the engine, and walked over to the rail, gazing at them. I felt the spirits of the Chacoan elders amongst them as they stared back at me silently in curiosity. Taking a deep breath, expanding my heart to love and oneness, I sent them, and perhaps my raven from the mesa, another message of deep gratitude. Seconds later, all of them were cawing back at me in a chorus. Tears again streamed down my cheeks as they seemingly acknowledged my message and returned it energetically and vocally.

Driving off, I felt disconnected from the modern 3-D world—but with a sense of connection to this dusty, enigmatic canyon in a way I would have never anticipated. Arriving back at my campsite I fired up my small camp stove to heat some tasty veggie chili. Soon the Milky Way galaxy and the Big Dipper, the Great Bear, and other constellations shone from above, filling me with a familiar expansive feeling, part of the universe. Crunching up some old newspaper and making a small firewood teepee, I kindled up a nice blaze, watching the embers dance towards the sky. Wow, what an amazing start to this trip. Who knows what else is to come in my next couple days here!

After burning through my small stack of pine, I crawled into my tent and began to meditate—lying down, with my Lemurian crystal on my forehead. About twenty minutes in, I suddenly had a vision of a Native American girl with long dark hair, likely in her early teens, placing the quartz crystal I'd just discovered. We stared into her eyes seeing a spiral in her pupils with a timeless essence. I could not fix the time she was there, but I'm sure it was from hundreds of years ago, when the Chacoans inhabited the area. She looked familiar, but I wasn't able to catch her name or if she was related to me in any way. I thanked the universe for this visual and continued my meditation, simply asking to become more connected to Chaco and the ancient energies and wisdom here.

Another ten minutes or so passed, when I was jolted by a surge of energy coming through the crystal on my Third Eye, which then traveled down my spine to my feet. My legs jerked as this happened several times, and it felt almost orgasmic, but flowed head to root rather than root to head. Between each surge of energy I breathed deeply and was then hit again and again. *OMG!! What is going on?* I'd had the occasional surge and flow like this before, but this was a tenfold repetition. I rode the waves of energy for an hour at least, then finally slipped into dream state till awakened by the morning sun.

Following my hearty oatmeal breakfast, I loaded up my daypack with water, snacks, and my flute to hike and meditate around more complexes. Parking at the trailhead, I walked down the canyon toward the Case Chiquita site. The hike began to feel surreal again as I walked down this slightly sandy trail, observing petroglyphs (rock carvings) as wells as the occasional raven flying overhead or perching on the canyon rim.

Arriving at Casa Chiquita, the site of a not-yet-formally-excavated house of roughly thirty-four ground-floor rooms, I found a shady spot to relax and meditate at, leaning against one of the ancient walls. The sandstone of the walls on Chaco sites have a unique pattern of thin, layered stone and mud holding them together. This characteristic masonry has helped the walls stand since their construction, 900–1150 AD.

Doorways of Pueblo Bonito, Chaco Canyon (photo by the author)

Wood for the beams over doorways, windows, and kivas was transported from the mountains more than sixty miles away. Archeologists drilled out small plugs of the wood to carbon date the sites and the types of trees used. It is estimated that 225,000 trees were harvested to build the Chaco Canyon structures.[9]

Cooling off in the shade and hydrating on this warm afternoon, I sat with legs crossed (easy pose), a crystal in either hand, to resonate with this site. The soft sand under my butt grounded me perfectly, and the cool stone wall at my back felt wonderful as I gently dropped into this thousand-year-old place. This time I began to feel energy coming through my tailbone or root chakra as I meditated. It was a light flow of energy without any shocks. The sensation was relaxing and nourishing. Meditating on the high mesa, and down lower by the wash, gave me a more diverse feel of the energies of Chaco. I ventured further west on the trail to see the red pictograph that likely documented the supernova seen by them in 1054.[10]

Fajada Butte at Chaco (photo by the author)

Chaco has always fascinated me for its archaeoastronomical alignments, especially on Fajada Butte, where the summer and winter solstices were monitored by the shadows cast from two large stones in front of a spiral petroglyph.

Discovering these alignments in 1977, Anna Sofaer was able to photograph them before the stones slipped out of position in the late '80s. This area has been closed since then, and I have been able to appreciate Fajada Butte only from a distance.

Sun Dagger by Francine Hart

The great kiva Casa Rinconada also has impressive alignments to the cardinal directions and a niche illuminated by the sun during the summer solstice:

> Casa Rinconada has an average interior diameter of 63 feet (19.2 m.). It contains all features generally associated with great kivas including a firebox, an inner bench, four large seating pits that served as roof supports, two masonry vaults/foot drums, and 34 niches encircling the great kiva. In addition, the kiva includes a 39-foot-long (12 m.) underground passage, three feet deep and almost three feet wide, entering the room from the northern antechamber. The underground passage would have allowed Chacoans, perhaps ritual specialists, to enter the great kiva unseen and then suddenly emerge.[11]

After this long day of hiking, I headed back to camp to cook dinner. Firing up my backpacking stove, I heated up some soup and relaxed in my camp chair. The temperature began to drop quickly after sunset, so I gathered up my remaining wood to make another fire in the pit. A couple gals walked by and asked if they could enjoy the fire with me. They were from nearby Albuquerque. "Of course, grab your chairs and come on over." We chatted for a good hour; I remember telling them the terrifying story of my son being bitten by a pit viper in Nepal and surviving, as well as having a short discussion of my work as a family medicine physician. After a couple drinks, they headed back to their campsite, and I slipped into my down bag, quickly falling asleep after a long day of exploring.

The following morning, I made a short visit to place crystals around the outside of the great kiva in the four directions, using my compass. I was by myself, so I played my flute, but stopped when I saw the gals from the campfire coming up the hill. After a short visit, I said goodbye and headed back to camp to pack up my gear and make the long drive home. As I drove down the wash-boarded dirt road I passed a hogan (a traditional Navajo dwelling) and reflected on my mystical journey. *Wow, how am I going to process this long weekend, and what does it all mean moving forward in my life's journey?*

Arriving back home in Denver, I explained what had happened broadly to the family, but felt it was another enigmantic trip challenging to convey.

Returning to the office Monday, I rocketed myself back into catch-up mode. Tuesday, I received a phone call from Steven, a psychologist residing in Albuquerque, New Mexico—a friend of an energy-medicine practitioner who worked in my office had connected me to him by phone several months ago, since we both shared interests in shamanism. He was planning on sending me a copy of his book on shamanic dreaming, so I figured he was simply calling about this.

His voice very excited, he said, "Fred, you're not going to believe this. I had lunch with a couple colleagues today. They began to talk about their adventures in Chaco Canyon last weekend and mentioned a fireside chat with a physician from Denver. I told them, 'I only know one physician in Denver and his name is Fred Grover.' They replied, *OMG, that's him. Look, here's his business card.* I smiled and couldn't believe it. I reached into my satchel and pulled out a large padded envelope with your name and address on it with my book enclosed. I told them, *I've been meaning to mail this to Fred for so long, and how crazy is it that this very day I decided to put it in the mail after lunch! Of course, here I am, having lunch with you after you just randomly met him. Now, that is synchronicity, brother!*

He said the gals' jaws dropped when he pulled the package out.

As I heard this, my jaw dropped too! *Wow, Steven, if that's not synchronicity and the universe talking, I don't know what is.* We both laughed, promising to meet soon after this unexplainable occurrence. I didn't have time to share the raven-and-crystal story over the phone that day, but I did later, when we met up for the first time. All I needed to really flip me out that day was to see a raven land on my windowsill with a crystal in its beak.

Chaco remains very special for me. I'll continue to visit this enchanted place whenever I can, awaiting my next enigmatic surprise . . .

Chapter 5:

Awakening the Divine Feminine Energy of Lake Titicaca

I t had been four years since my last visit to Peru, in 2011. I'd continued my meditative work and found myself traveling deep into shamanic dream states, especially when I combined sound therapy and sacred geometry. Modifications to my meditation space in 2015 helped me achieve deeper states more rapidly, and I even experienced periodic out-of-body spirit travel. Combining the sound lounger and a sacred geometric 3-D star form (by Metaforms), suspended on a cord above my Third Eye, further enhanced the energy flow. I experienced myself opening up my luminous light body, and would then feel light energy flowing freely like a river into my Third Eye, descending all the way down to my root chakra and feet. It was similar to what a single quartz crystal could do, but amplified three times, with the form just touching the Third Eye region of my forehead.

Experimenting, I found that adding four crystals to the form, wired in with copper, further increased its ability to channel in energy and connections to the cosmos.

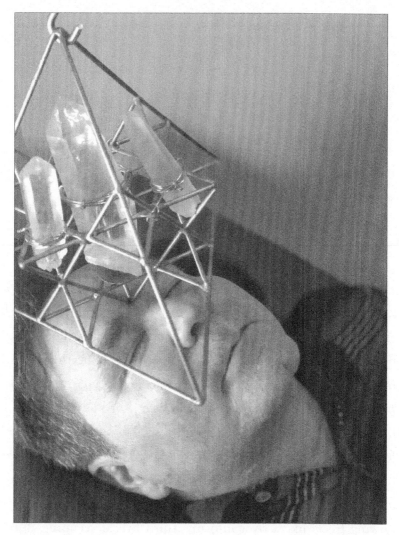

Author with 3-D star and Lemurian crystals (photo by Keaton Grover); 3-D star crafted by Gregory Hoag; see: iconnect2all.com for this geometric shape, the Unity grid, and others.

I continued to dive deeper into sound healing, resonating frequency-based music, such as binaural beats or mantra music, to aid in balancing my energy body and opening my chakras while on the sound lounger. Later, purchasing the elaborate Pleiadian

Connection Portal, I placed it in the windowsill next to the sound lounger. This was conceived by Christine Day and then constructed by Gregory Hoag, sacred Metaforms geometer from Lyons Colorado. As they describe it, "This powerful sacred geometric antenna system includes the Pleiadian structure; spinning Metatron's Cube; toroidal ring with caduceus coil and alchemical mixture of various charged crystals."[12]

Pleiadian Portal in author's meditation space, designed by Christine Day and constructed by Greg Hoag; see: iconnect2all.com for this and other Metaforms.

Finding this alchemy of geometry, sound, and crystals to optimize the meditative field took time. It made me contemplate the geometries of the pyramids, Stonehenge, Angkor Wat, and many other ancient sites that tapped into the field on a much larger and more complicated scale. While my space is far from having the resonate and geometric alignments of the Great Pyramid of Giza's Kings Chamber, it does contain geometries aligned with it, as well as the capability of resonating the F-sharp tone found in the chamber. Anyone can create a powerful meditative space, but I feel it best to incorporate what resonates with your energy body. Create a space for yourself that can help you travel out of body through higher dimensions flowing through surrounding portals just as one navigates a river in flow with the elements.

One evening while doing a longer, three-hour meditation, dialing in these various tools, I could see myself soaring south over Central America and eventually found myself hovering over what came to me as Lake Titicaca. The eastern half is in Bolivia, with the Andes flowing water into it, and the western half is in Peru. Observing the sacred lake, I felt it was depleted of energy. I couldn't perceive if this was from pollution or a lack of attention to its energetic needs, which were once blessed by Incas, and the Pre-Inca temples of Tiwanaku and Puma Punku to the south. There was a glow of light from its deepest point, but I sensed it was much more radiant in the past. According to Pre-Incan and Incan legend, Viracocha, the creator god, emerged from the waters of Titicaca to create mankind and all else in the world.

It is described as the cradle of the Incan civilization.

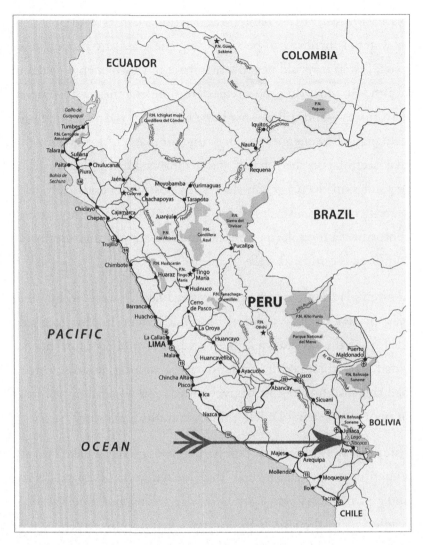

Lake Titicaca location in South America (iStock)

As I observed the lake in my deep state, I had the insight that it needed some kind of energy boost to help it regain its life force energy, or prana. Many shamans see this deep, high-altitude lake surrounded by mountains as the representation of the divine feminine, or womb of Mother Earth, with Mount Everest representing the divine masculine. The ongoing exploitation of our planet for fossil fuels, habitat destruction via fires, and polluting of waters is believed to be impacting the energetic properties of Gaia, just as it would negatively impact our own energy field and health. By nurturing the divine feminine energies at this sacred lake, it was—and still is—my hope to counter the more predominate masculine energies endangering our planet. Again, while this may seem far-fetched, Earth is our mothership and her health is beyond skin deep. . I can do what's possible energetically with placements, but also doing my part by minimizing my carbon footprint via my solar powered home and supporting sustainable solutions is critical as well.

Contemplating how to help this sacred lake, it came to me to at least place a large crystal deep into her waters. I didn't have any idea what this would look like or when it would occur, but decided to meditate on it further over the coming months. Once I had this insight, my spirit travel ended, and I found myself back in my room, feeling I'd left a timeless multidimensional space.

Later that week, I told the family that I was going to Lake Titicaca sometime in the near future. They looked at me like I was crazy, and all I could say was, *I am called to go there, and I must go.* This magical spot, the largest freshwater lake in South America, is at an elevation of 12,000 feet and flanked to the east by the rugged Bolivian Andes mountain range.

Many meditations later, I had another insight—that for it to be effective, I should amplify the power of the Lemurian crystal to be placed in the lake. The sacred geometric form of Gregory Hoag's Unity Grid I'd been meditating with came intuitively as the perfect form to alchemize with the crystal to be placed inside it. According to him, this spherical shape contains sixty inter-connected triangles, each having the same angles as the triangular faces of the Great Pyramid of Giza. It is the higher order of two platonic solids, the dodecahedron and icosahedron, which are woven together forming a cross in the phi ratio relationship. The form resonates with DNA, amplifying love, compassion, gratitude and our connection to oneness. Surrounding the large crystal with this geometric field would allow the water to connect to it in a radial fashion, creating a dynamic ball of energy deep within the lake center. (See the photo on page 72.) My initial view of the lake in the shamanic dream showed a dim white light being emitted, almost like from a flashlight trying to shine forth to the surface. I envisioned her regaining a full-spectrum, highly energized, lighthouse-intensity rainbow-light spectrum that had been present in the distant past. Somewhat analogous to a Tibetan monk achieving the Rainbow Body, this sacred lake needed rainbow-light energy filling it from her deepest depths to the shores, the streams feeding her, the mountains, and beyond. Creating this field might help purify the waters and protect the endangered species of frogs and other creatures endemic to this embryonic-like lake. Most importantly, I visualized it radiating the divine feminine energy to the entire planet, countering predominant dark energies of greed and power arising from out-of-balance masculine energies. I recognized the disruption it might create by threatening masculine energy fields on Gaia, but realized this rebalancing was past due.

Seeking further input on my trip to Peru, I sat down for dinner with my friend Jonette Crowley, author of *The Eagle and the Condor* and a well-known channeler, to get her thoughts on timing and a few other questions. After describing what I had downloaded and planned so far, she felt the timing should be during the upcoming blood moon. It's called a blood moon due to the reddish hue that occurs from the refraction of sunlight around the Earth's atmosphere during a total lunar eclipse. Of course, there are energetic and spiritual alignments happening with this event too. The other element she felt was needed was a blue or turquoise rock to surround the Lemurian crystal. I felt into that more, asking her if our local amazonite rock from nearby Teller County, Colorado, would be a good fit. "Yes!" she said. *Excellent*, I said. *I love its Caribbean blue color and feel it will help connect the sphere more to the waters.*

The Denver rock-and-gem show had just passed; I'd missed that opportunity. Calling a few shops, I was bummed to hear that no one had amazonite. As a final effort, I decided to personally drop into the SpiritWays store not far from my house. Looking around, I saw a large selection of gems, but no amazonite. Rather than walking out the door, I asked the owner if she had any in back storage, and she answered, "That's crazy you're asking me for it. A gal came in this morning with a box of amazonite, seeing if I wanted to purchase them. I declined, thinking I wouldn't be able to sell them. She told me she'd collected the pieces on her own, years ago, and felt the urge to let them go to someone else. Almost like she received a message to let them go. Luckily, she left her number, so I'll call her tomorrow and see if she still has them.

"What do you want them for?" she asked.

Well, I'm not putting them on a bookshelf, but doing something a little different. My intention is to place them with a large crystal in-

side a bronze sacred-geometric sphere deep in waters of Lake Titicaca in South America to help rekindle the divine feminine energies there.

She stared at me like I was from another planet, followed by tears rolling down her cheeks. "OMG, this sounds magical. I'll call her in the morning and let you know what she says." The following morning, she called to tell she'd bring them in. At the store I found the most perfect pieces to go inside the sphere with the crystal. I thought to myself: *Wow, this is synchronicity flowing again, and that these beautiful pieces were hand collected by a woman and released to the universe by her intuition is unbelievable. Knowing that she had come by earlier that same day to let them go after holding them for years was even more auspicious.*

Greg had his artisans build a large, basketball-sized bronze Unity Grid for me to place the crystal and amazonite into. It was much three times bigger than imagined, so I was a bit worried that I'd have to put it in my checked bag. I secured the crystals and amazonite with copper wire at the base, then wired in a few other items, including a small bronze Buddha, a Dorje (small symbolic Buddhist piece), a cross, and a quetzal (sacred bird, representing the rainbow feathered serpent, Quetzalcoatl, a Maya and Aztec deity). *Wow, this is really coming together! Somehow, I need to charge this up ceremonially.*

I called Greg and asked him for ideas. He said, "Fred, as a matter a fact, I have a shaman friend, Daniel Gutierrez, coming out from California next weekend. Perhaps we could do a ceremony on our property with him if that feels right." Daniel Gutierrez is the bestselling author of *Radical Mindfulness*. Thinking to myself, I thought, well of course he's coming out next weekend! Briefly pausing, I replied, *That sounds excellent, Greg! Lets make it happen.* I called around; by the weekend we had close to twelve people show up. Forming a circle near a sacred tree on the ridge, just above his house, we all sent intentions to charge the sphere to create a powerful activation, once placed in the lake. Holding hands in a circle, we called in the four directions, and each of us sent a prayer and intention to help activate the Unity Grid even more. We then followed this by playing our hand drums in unison for a while, spiraling this energy into the cosmos. We headed down the trail to Greg's house below, and I thanked him and Gail for hosting the ceremony, and everyone that showed up to amplify the sphere and hold space.

Greg Hoag, the author, and Jonette Crowley with Unity Grid just after ceremony. Activated shamanically by group on Greg's land near Lyons, Colorado, and facilitated by Daniel Gutierrez

Logistically speaking, I had booked my flights and located the places to stay when arriving in Peru. I was concerned about hiring a boat and not being able to communicate with a local on this unusual mission that brought me out to the wide-open waters on the blood moon to drop the sphere. I decided to email Allyson—who runs a shamanic retreat center near Pisac—having done an ayahuasca ceremony with her shaman a few years prior. She emailed back, saying call me. On an internet-based call later that week, she said, "Fred, I don't believe you are telling me you'd like to place a crystal in Lake Titicaca. About ten years ago, I placed a crystal between Island of the Sun and Moon, and that night we did ceremony on Island of the Sun with my Shipibo shaman husband. While deep in the journey I was told that in the future someone would contact me to place another crystal in the lake. I'm sure that's you!"

Taking some deep breaths and processing what she'd just said, I thought: *Wow, OK, here is the universe responding once again!* "Allyson, any chance you could meet me in late September for the blood moon to do this placement, help translate, and do ceremony?" She had clients coming then but said, "Let me see if someone can cover our center. This is too important to miss and I'm happy to help you with logistics. Let's meet in Copacabana, Bolivia, then take a ferry to Island of the Sun." A few emails later, and I had set up flights for her; her husband, Loyver; and Ron, their assistant. She would bring ayahuasca for a sacred ceremony after the placement.

Time for departure approached quickly; I began to organize. Looking at the large sphere, I realized it was too big, and likely too weird an object, to clear airport security. I decided to wrap it in some T-shirts, then pack it within a plastic box and check it inside my large duffle bag. I was concerned it might get crushed, or taken out by security, but sent the deepest prayers for it to arrive safely. With all the extra crystals, water purifier, clothes, etc., my bag was just under fifty pounds.

Arriving in Lima, late at night, I stayed at the airport hotel to quickly catch my flight next morning to the town of Juliaca, located near Puno and the shores of the lake.

Arriving early for check-in, I found the line insanely long. Waiting a good forty-five minutes in line, I was lucky enough to have an angelic representative from LATAM Airlines ask my departure time. Looking at it, she quickly brought me to the front for check-in, which meant I didn't miss my flight. Boarding at the last moment, I took deep breaths and sent gratitude to the universe. Funny how deep breaths are becoming more and more of a thing as I travel through these 3-D fields into interdimensional fields. It's almost like me preparing to make a surface dive while snorkeling helping me flow with from the air, into the liquid magic of the reef, sea turtles and fish deep below me.

Landing in the windy, dusty town of Juliaca, I walked across the tarmac to the lone small-baggage carousel. Watching the luggage circle around the clunky carousel, I saw the locals and just a few tourists grab their bags. The carousel was empty except for a couple boxes, and I never saw my bag come out. Big sigh. Guess it got lost or didn't make it on the flight. Not good. My pulse climbed, and as I anxiously thought about my bag being lost.

While I'd packed some nice back-up crystals in my daypack, I couldn't imagine not being able to place the sphere. I sent out some prayers as I watched the carousel turn and then suddenly heard some luggage being thrown onto the belt from outside. To my surprise it emerged from the flaps onto the carousel. *OMG, there is a god!* I could see the box with the sphere was still in the duffle, apparently intact. I set the heavy duffle on the ground beside me, sending gratitude for its safe arrival. My pulse had normalized by now, after that traumatic event, and as I was getting ready to walk over to the local bus area, a gal tapped me on the shoulder. *Where are you heading to?* she said.

"Well, I'm trying to make it down to Copacabana, Bolivia, then planning to head to Island of the Sun. How about you?" *That's funny, I'm heading there too.* "Very cool," I said. "I was planning on taking the local bus, but if we can hire a taxi, perhaps we could make it in four hours instead of eight and share the cost. What's your name?" *Shelley.* "OK, Shelley, are you in for this road trip?" *Yes!*

Asking around, it took a while to negotiate a good price with a driver willing to make the hundred-mile trip to the border of Bolivia. We found a nice guy who spoke a little English, loaded our bags in the trunk, jumped in, and headed out. Shelley looked a little younger than me; she clearly had an adventurous spirit like me. Her medium-length curly hair with shades of grey amongst darker brown gave her a beautiful, natural appearance.

Thinking I was simply sharing a ride with someone interested in the typical sightseeing, I looked her in the eyes. "What brings you here?" I asked. Expecting something more like, *I want to see this and that*, I heard her reply, "I am here to help activate my divine feminine energy." Another OMG/Holy F moment, where I kept my calm and replied, "So how do you plan to do that?" Well, while working in a meditative circle with my shaman group in Squamish, BC, I told them I was drawn to going to Peru to help fulfill this intention. I have booked a few excursions to see Machu Picchu and Salkantay, but everything else is open. They told me to minimize my planning and to simply fly down to Lake Titicaca and let spirit show me the way. We do our meditative circles with a mesa. Do you know what a mesa is?"

Hearing all of this, I didn't know how to begin my answer—honestly overwhelmed at what I'd just heard. Taking a few deep breaths to process her revelation, I responded, *OK, I am going to tell you something you may not believe. The large duffle bag in the trunk contains a sphere with crystals inside it that I plan to place in the waters off Island of the Sun soon to help activate the divine feminine energy of the lake and mother Gaia. I feel there's no mistake that we are in this car together.*

"No way," she said. "Are you really planning to do that!!?"

As crazy as it sounds, yes. I'm actually meeting a gal with her shaman husband from the Pisac area in Copacabana tonight. You are welcome to join us on this journey if you feel it is in flow with your work. One other interesting detail is that I am also a mesa carrier. I know very few mesa carriers and find it so curious that you are one too! We chatted the whole way down, and before we arrived at our final destination, she let me know that she wanted to join our group journey to the island. After crossing the Bolivian border, then grabbing another cab for a short ride to Copacabana, we walked down the beach to the ecolodge, where the others were waiting. The group was excited to hear the story and have her coming along.

Unity Grid being activated on north end of Island of the Sun at Chincana ruins (photo by the author)

The next morning we set out on a small boat to Island of the Sun (Isla del Sol). Arriving at the pier on the north end, we were met by a young girl who invited us to stay at her place nearby. We felt good about it, so we followed her to the small family-run lodge where her mother set us up in a few small rooms with amazing views of the Andes mirrored in the crystal-blue lake. Midafternoon we made a nice hike, dodging some pigs and goats along the way, to the Inca ruins of Roca Sagrada and held a small ceremony at the nearby Chincana ruins to bless the sphere one more time.

Looking to the north off the tip of Isla del Sol, I could see three small islands, each about fifty yards in diameter.

Author with the three small islands in far background (photo by Shelley Genovese)

Together they formed a triangle, and I felt the most powerful location to place the sphere would be deep in the waters beyond the island at the more distant apex. Back in the village in the eve, Allyson spoke with a few local fisherman and helped me hire a boat.

The next morning we boarded the small covered boat early to avoid the higher winds and waves later in the day. Loyver (Allyson's husband and shaman) brought his flute, and I carried the Unity Grid sphere on board for its final voyage. The captain was a friendly guy, and I was bummed I wasn't fluent in Spanish to converse with him myself. Allyson relayed the navigational plan to him and we headed out of the small harbor. Coming around the north point of the island, the captain took us over a submerged archway from an ancient ruin. I was excited that we could distinctly see it just ten to fifteen feet below the stern in the clear blue waters. I happened to have a few extra Lemurians in my daypack, so I pulled out the largest and dropped it right over the arch. My impression is that this region sunk under the water, as the overall lake water level has been receding, not rising.

We continued north, where the wind picked up and the swells increased. When Loyver became nauseous, we stopped for a while on one of the small islands. Hiking around a bit, we identified the foundations of several ancient structures and placed a few crystals nearby prior to boarding our small boat. . Loyver, had quickly resolved his nausea so we untied the boat and headed back out into the rough waters.

Our Lake Titicaca Unity Grid deployment boat! Tied up on small central island just in front of deep waters for placement (photo by the author)

Our captain directed the small vessel towards the deep blue, just a few hundred yards beyond this apex island. Loyver played his flute, and we all held the sphere before I gently launched it into the azure waters. Watching it sink out of sight, I continued to hold the prayer to enable it to bless the lake and regenerate and amplify the divine feminine, or goddess, energies of the past.

Looking out over the water and listening to Loyver playing his flute, I suddenly saw a smooth two-foot-wide line form, extending all the way across the water from where the sphere was dropped to the shore of Isla del Sol. This was a distinct linear line, not from the wind or a boat wake. All I could detect was that the placement had created an energetic line all the way to the north point of the island. We watched in disbelief for a few minutes as it remained intact, unaffected by the choppy windblown water. Sitting there in the rocking boat, looking at Shelley and the others' radiant energy, seemed both timeless and surreal. Not my typical day in the office. *Wow, this really happened.* As I brought myself back to the moment, the captain fired up the outboard engine and we headed back to the village with the wind on our backs.

The evening of the blood moon, Loyver and Allyson opened the shamanic circle for us in one of the larger rooms at the lodge. We made our intentions one by one, going round the circle. Mine was simply to have the sphere radiate light energy through the sacred lake and for this to pulse out a nurturing feminine energy to create a balanced yin/yang planetary energy, clearing the toxic masculine energy. They then prepared and blessed the ayahuasca plant medicine brought all the way from the Amazonian rainforest of Peru.

Ayahuasca tea is brewed in the rainforest by breaking up and boiling the sacred vine (Banisteriopsis caapi) and typically adding leaves from the chacruna shrub (Psychotria viridis) that contains DMT (dimethyltryptamine). DMT, an entheogen, has a stimulating effect on the pineal gland, the deep interior organ in the brain often identified with the Third Eye in the Hindu chakra system. The Greek word *entheogen* means "generating the divine within."

We each drank a small cup of the bitter tea and listened to Loyver singing icaros, playing his guitar. Icaros, songs composed by the Shipibo of the Amazon, are designed to help activate ayahuasca so it can do the deeper healing. Within an hour we began to feel and see the psychedelic visions of this powerful vine. This night and on many other journeys with this plant medicine, I've seen the color and geometry amplified during the singing of icaros. In a sense, the music appears to be assisting visually in the weaving of higher-dimensional geometries. What I consider to be at least 5-D, and something so complex I could not re-create it even with a high-end graphic program. Fractalized geometry is often seen in the 2-D art of visionary artist Alex Grey, and can also be seen in the 3-D at places such as the Alhambra (palace) in its Moorish art in the ceiling.

Fractal geometry at Alhambra (Shutterstock)

My journey began with this colorful geometry on this blood moon night, then shifted to a visual of the Unity Grid and crystals glowing brightly on the floor of Lake Titicaca. I could clearly see it beaming energy and rainbow light to the entire lake, up into the tributary streams flowing down from the Andes. The apus (spirits of the mountains) were connecting to the field as well. While still in this zone of limited consciousness, I sent the intention to spread this light around the world like a band of light that went to the North and South poles; then visualized the light spinning clockwise around Gaia, sending love, compassion, and healing light to all. Soon after, I shifted into a deeper state and felt myself traveling into the cosmos. I was about to experience the wildest ayahuasca journey ever.

I found myself on a spaceship, undergoing heart surgery! *WTF?* I lay awake on the table with my chest cracked opened, as alien-like greys proceeded to do what appeared to be microsurgery on my heart. I'd heard of, but had never experienced, shamanic dissection. During what seemed like hours, I watched them do surgery on me. Telling them I needed to return to Earth intact and healthy, I heard: "Don't worry. We are simply making some energetic enhancements to your heart. All will be fine." I did my best to allow this healing work to occur, making sure I didn't get any "implants," which some of my more cosmic friends had warned me about.

Within a couple hours, I believe, I opened my eyes and could see the full blood moon rising over the Andes.

Blood moon rising over the Bolivian Andes and Lake Titicaca (photo by the author)

Its blood-orange color and amplified size was a powerful sight to behold. Loyver was playing his flute now, and as I looked out over the moonlit lake, I became very nauseous. Walking outside to the deck of this second floor, I gazed at the lake, gripped the rail, and intensely purged to the ground below. Luckily no one was walking by! I felt a clearing of dark energy from my energy body, followed by an infusion of healing light from Lake Titicaca, the Andes Mountains, and the moon rising in the sky. Allyson came out to help me flow this energy and breathe through this purge, balancing my energy and helping me ground out. Late that night I fell asleep, still feeling the medicine work through me in dream space.

The next morning we integrated what had come in for us during the ceremony and discussed what we had felt and experienced. I took the boat back to Copacabana with the group, saying goodbye to Allyson and her crew as they returned to the Sacred Valley. Shelley had decided to come along with me on a side trip to the mysterious pre-Inca site of Tiwanaku and Puma Punku before heading off. After a long bus ride, hiring a private driver, we arrived at Tiwanaku, frequently discussed in the TV series *Ancient Aliens* with Giorgio A. Tsoukalos; it has the most intricate laser-like carvings in granite that to this day can't be reproduced with our laser and high-tech stone-cutting tools.

To help us understand this complex site, we hired a local guide on arrival. One of the most intriguing areas was a rectangular subterranean temple that has close to one hundred carved stone heads of various ethnic groups/races inserted in the four walls.

Subterranean temple at Tiwanaka with carved heads of ethnic groups from around the world (photo by the author)

The guide pointed out the local Tiwanakan heads, and African-American, Asian, and others, but one type was by far the most interesting. There was an alien-like head on each of the four walls, contrasted with just one head of most other races.

Alien head in the subterranean temple (photo by the author)

Clearly, in the subterranean temple this race played a prominent role. I decided to ask our guide, an answer I already knew, just to hear his reply: *So, do you think aliens, or beings from other planets, helped construct this complex site?* "Well, of course! I am of Tiwanakan descent from thousands of years and many generations. Our people know and believe that we had help from visitors from the stars." *Perfect*, I thought. *He could have hedged a bit, but this was the most clear-cut, confirming reply I could have asked for.*

Walking around, he showed us the powerful Gate of the Sun, with the creator deity Viracocha centered on the arch.

The Spanish moved this sacred gate to the capital of La Paz sometime back; it fortunately was returned to Tiwanaku temple years later. Sadly, they placed it in the corner of the temple rather than in its original more powerful central position. I often wonder if it was placed back in the temple out of its original alignment to avoid re-activating its powers. It has always looked and intuitively feels like a portal to me. Some day if they relocate the gate to its original position, I'll be sure to return!

Author behind the Gate of the Sun (photo by Shelley Genovese)

In the central part of the temple it is a large square-shaped magnetic stone. As our guide placed a compass on it; the compass needle spun. *Wow, I've never seen that.* I was feeling inclined to sit and meditate on the stone, so I asked him if we could do that. Giving a thumbs up, he headed off for a break and agreed to meet us in thirty minutes. Amazingly, there was no one else on the site except for an elderly local woman sitting in the shade, knitting a sweater. Shelley and I decided to sit half lotus on a large, black magnetic stone to feel into the energies of this temple. During the twenty-minute meditation, we felt an intense flow of kundalini from our root chakras through our crowns. I had to work with my breath to tolerate the intensity. Towards the end we both opened our eyes spontaneously, looking at each other, intuitively sharing how profound the experience was. We laughed saying it felt like we had both orgasmed simultaneously on the rock together. I'm sure if we had the place to ourselves and could make love there something magical would have happened! Most intriguing was when I turned around, the elderly lady was behind us and simply said, beaming, "Muy bueno." It was as if she were there as a temple elder, observing us and the field we created and vortexed into while on this energized magnetic rock. Following this, we placed a few small Lemurians in cracks around the temple to honor it and rejoined our guide.

On the short drive over to Puma Punku, we marveled at the amazing multilayered megalithic stone carvings, especially the so-called "H-blocks."

The stones are so scattered at this site, one has to wonder what cataclysmic event leveled it. Using computer models, including 3-D printed miniatures, archeologists continue to theorize about its original configuration and purpose. One thing is clear from visiting this site, viewing the precision stone-cutting and the large megalithic stones that had to be transported for miles. They must have had help from an extremely advanced group of stone movers, masons, and stone cutters—most likely visitors from far away. At the very least, they were lent some impressive power tools and levitation devices!

The H-blocks of Puma Punku (photo by the author)

Making the long journey back to Puno, Peru, and seeing the floating islands of Uros was impressive, but felt very touristy. Feeling
starved that evening, Shelley and I enjoyed a nice dinner free of
guinea pigs in Puno, and then returned to our shared room that
evening.

Our sexual and energetic attractions had been building over the
last few days to a point that we both could feel the tension building. A palpable deeper connection to her from my 3rd eye down to
my root chakra needed to be more intimately shared between us.

Laying in my bed, feeling this building tension, I was elated to
hear her say; "Come over here and join me for a breathwork meditation".

We both sat in half lotus staring in each other's eyes. "Follow my
breath" she said. Following her deep and rapid holotropic pat-

tern, I began to feel my crown chakra feeling lighter and tingling in my hands. She then held my hands creating an intense flow of energy traveling up my shoulders and down to my root chakra.

"Let's bring more light from our crown chakras into our hearts" she said, "then use our breaths to flow it through all of our chakras." Visualizing myself connecting to the constellation of Pleiades the light began to spiral and expand through my light body. At this point a resonate field of energy morphing between the two of us began to form.

Amplifying and flowing this cosmic light more into my root chakra, I could feel her root chakra pulsing more toward mine.

My root chakra was now on fire, and I could feel myself so aroused that I could barely stand it!

We slowed our breathing, then embraced each other, followed by deep passionate kisses that coupled us even deeper. Holding her forehead next to mine our 3rd eyes joined together creating a tingling sensation followed by another wave of energy flowing down to my root chakra. I ran my fingertips down the curve of her spine to the tip of her tail bone, flowing her energy more to her root.

Slowly she pulled of her shirt unveiling her beautiful breasts. A flickering candle on the bedside table illuminated her nipples perfectly. Seeing they desired attention, I ran my tongue down to circle and then kiss them making them firm. Taking my shirt off, we embraced each other feeling our hearts pulsing rapidly between our naked chests.

In seconds we were fully unclothed, and she was on top of me.

OMG, I thought, this is some serious divine feminine energy!! Wasn't expecting this. Perhaps she's been supercharged by the Lake Titicaca ceremony and the magnetic rock!

Positioning herself over me, she slowly descended her yoni allowing me to go deep inside her. Holding herself there, she began to slowly ride me. Pure, slow, torture. Feeling an urge to explode I took some deep breaths and held on to her hips. Alternating between holding her breasts and her hips, she then increased her tempo, and began to glide her clitoris more intensely along my mons pubis. She began to moan with each descent, and I responded by thrusting more upwards feeling myself go even deeper into her. She was so dripping wet now that I could feel her wetness cascading down my shaft and between my legs.

A could sense a tantric flow of energy spiraling and pulsing between us as our root and second chakras pulsed with a growing sphere of energy. Soon I could feel and see it spiraling our kundalini light up through and out of our crown chakras.

We felt ourselves then transitioning into a vibrational field of oneness. The unity grid on the floor of Lake Titicaca flashed into my consciousness during this. Squeezing her sweet ass tightly, and pulling her in tight, I released with one of the most intense, long orgasms I'd ever experienced. She came just after I released, and I had a vision of a burst of energy flowing from us to heal and balance mother Gaia. Never had I imagined that this journey to place a crystal in Lake Titicaca would also lead to such a powerful union of divine feminine and masculine energies to help heal Gaia.

The next morning, I gave Shelley a big hug as she headed out to fly back to the north to visit Mount Salkantay, Machu Picchu, and other sacred sites. "I am called to Mount Salkantay to further activate my divine feminine energy" said Shelley. How perfect I thought as I looked in her beautiful eyes. Darn, wish I could venture there too, but both of our travel plans were more structured moving forward.

Handing her most of my remaining Lemurian crystals, I asked that she place them in the sacred spots where she was called to. Her auric field radiated as she waved. It was such a strange good-bye. I felt in my heart that I would see her again sometime soon. Our work together was not over. I thanked the universe for her existence, and for her synchronistic ability to show up and participate in the placement of the crystal at Lake Titicaca and so much more....

A Quetzal connecting the energies of Machu Picchu, Palenque, and Chaco as envisioned by the author and drawn by commissioned artist Danielle Lanslots

Chapter 6:

The Crystal Skulls, Energizing the rainbow-light field of Quetzalcoatl

Maya iconography and pyramids continued to enter my consciousness sporadically during meditations, sometimes with the beautiful quetzal bird flowing streaming light energies between crystals I'd placed in sacred areas. The image came up so much that I sketched my vision and then commissioned my artist friend Danielle Lanslots to try to create something beautiful with sacred geometry incorporated into the quetzal.

Spending a weekend at the Arise summer music festival, I was further drawn into the patterns of the Maya, Aztec, and Toltec by a few artists who displayed their works in the large tent gallery overlooking the music venue below. Later that summer I immersed myself even more with Mayan "visionary"-type art at Denver's First Friday Art Walks on Santa Fe Boulevard. I began to wonder if the pattern recognition of artists connecting to this ancient culture was being enhanced by ayahuasca or other psychoactive plant medicines. Having seen these patterns in meditating with shamanic medicine, I had often wanted to pick up a brush and try to re-create at least a glimpse. Candidly to one artist, I said, *Have you used ayahuasca or psilocybin to create this art?* Smiling back, he said, "Yes, in fact, not only did it draw me into the mysteries of the ancients, like the Maya, but it helped invigorate my own creativity. Looking at Maya artforms served as a stimulating base template to expand from." Seeing this art and hearing from artists further enticed me to expand into the realms of the Maya.

Attending a meditation circle not long after this music fest and art event, I offered some energy work to a friend. I too love to receive energy work from others, especially when I'm feeling a bit off-kilter.

She had been struggling with various issues and desired to balance and connect her chakras. After assessing her energy field, I placed some Lemurian crystals on her second, third, and fourth chakras and then decided to channel the Maya feathered serpent, Quetzalcoatl. This deity of light, God of the Morning Star, is of Mesoamerican (Mayan/Aztec/Toltec) origin, with complex roles that include contributing to fertility, agriculture, and healing; inventing books and the calendar; and becoming a patron of Mesoamerican priests.[13]

Some Mormons feel that Quetzalcoatl is synonymous with Jesus, as stated by their third president, John Taylor: "The story of the life of the Mexican divinity, Quetzalcoatl, closely resembles that of the Savior; so closely, indeed, that we can come to no other conclusion than that Quetzalcoatl and Christ are the same being."[14]

As I connected to the healing energies of the feathered serpent I could feel more than usual light flowing through my palms and fingertips. As I sent light from the tip of my right index finger, touching the Third Eye region of her forehead, my friend jolted, saying, "OMG, Fred. I'm seeing rainbow light running through my body! How are you doing that?" *I'm not exactly sure, I'm simply connecting to some Mayan healing energies, with the intent to send you light and heal whatever is needed in you.*

As I continued to flow rainbow light energy through her, she began to feel cleared of unwanted dark energies and felt the voids filled with this healing energy. I helped guide her on a meditation to bring this light in on her own through her crown and to every molecule in her body, infusing herself with light whenever possible, to sustain a balanced field.

Flowing these energies and seeing the images meditatively, I felt drawn to return to the Yucatán, to discover more hidden mysteries of the Maya. Following online the teachings of Miguel Angel Vergara, a scholar and teacher of Mayan shamanic traditions, I decided to reach out to him and see if he'd be willing to guide a small private group in February 2018. Receiving a thumbs-up from his team, we began planning a trip that would start at Chichén Itzá on our own, then later in the week meet up with him at Uxmal near Mérida.

Meditatively I began to have frequent, clear insights that I needed to place a crystal or something else powerful in the cenotes of Chichén Itzá to reawaken the energies of Quetzalcoatl (Kukulkan). Cenotes are formed when due to erosion a surface layer of limestone collapses, which then exposes groundwater or an aquifer. We often call these sinkholes in America. The Maya used these as a water source and also as a place to make offerings to the gods. Here's a good explanation of why these cenotes are important:

> The town of Chichen-Itza was established during the Classic period close to two natural cavities (**cenotes** or **chenes**), which gave the town its name "At the edge of the well of the Itzaes." The **cenotes** facilitated tapping the underground waters of the area.[15]

As I tapped into this more, crystal skulls kept coming into my meditative field. I'd never been a huge fan of crystal skulls, unlike some of my spiritual friends, and often found them kind of creepy. But not wanting to be judgmental, I maintained an open mind to see what further details would emerge. As I was taking a shower one morning it hit me so fast there might as well have been a fiber optic cable plugged into my head! I was to place two crystal skulls into each cenote, with a Lemurian seed crystal wrapped together with them. One skull would be rose quartz, resonating with feminine energies, and the other lapis lazuli, resonating with masculine energies.

Wow, crazy that this came through as I showered before heading off to a busy day, seeing patients. Given my limited time to prepare, I looked online for the skulls and ordered six each of two different types delivered to my office. I had plenty of Lemurian seed crystals in stock in a box under my bed. A week later the package arrived, with an invoice for twelve skulls. But interestingly enough, inside was a total of thirteen. Hmm, that's cool.

Wonder why they gave me a bonus skull. Thinking about it for a while, I remembered watching the *Indiana Jones and the Kingdom of the Crystal Skull* 2008 movie. How many skulls did Steven Spielberg have in the film? Thirteen, of course! Becoming more curious, I researched how many life-sized Mesoamerican crystal skulls exist, based on legend. Thirteen was the number, and some Maya elders say there are four sets of thirteen. Continued controversy exists regarding the authenticity of some crystal skulls in museums and the total number that exist.

But one that has particularly captured the public imagination is the Mitchell-Hedges crystal skull, reportedly discovered by Anna, the daughter of British adventurer and author F. A. Mitchell-Hedges, under an altar at the top of a pyramid in the Mayan city of Lubaantun, Belize. Evaluation by Hewlett-Packard labs in Santa Clara in 1970 showed this very hard crystal was polished beyond what we could accomplish with modern tools and without evidence of machine markings.[16] New Age theorists cite Maya legend claiming that when the original thirteen skulls of ET origin are united, there will be an awakening of knowledge from the entire universe.[17]

Whether the arrival of thirteen skulls instead of twelve was an accident or the universe taunting me more, I will never know. Regardless, they were all coming with me.

Needing others to help with this challenging journey, I reached out to my friend Terry, who had assisted me by doing several amazing placements in Cambodia around Angkor Wat a year prior. She and others would join us on our spiritual journey in the Yucatán. Terry has an innate ability to feel the sacred energies beyond 3-D and into the multiverse. Having her goddess-like energy and skills on this trip seemed paramount in making these sacred placements, and balancing the masculine energies.

After arriving in Cancún we made our way to archeological site of Chichén Itzá by car in a couple hours and stayed at the historic Mayaland Hotel, built on the periphery of the ruins in the 1920s. Small pyramids even exist on the grounds there. The one thousand acres of Chichén Itzá Archaeological Park is now a UNESCO World Heritage Site—a central feature being "one of the New Seven Wonders of the World, El Castillo" (the Kukulkan pyramid).[18] Chichén Itzá was built by the Maya during the Late Classic period, likely beginning in 750 AD, and the Kukulkan pyramid is near this central site. We timed our arrival to coincide with the total lunar eclipse of January 31, 2018, also known as a super Blue Moon.

After getting settled at the Mayaland hotel, we gathered in the evening to arrange our skulls in a circle around a large skull named Rosa that Terry had brought. This skull had been in circle and charged by the famous life-sized "Max" crystal skull, discovered in Guatemala, so our intention was to connect our thirteen skulls to Rosa and the energies of Max, prior to placing them. Max, internationally famous, the subject of documentaries, is considered one of the thirteen crystal skulls of the Maya; it's estimated to be over ten thousand years old.[19] Holding a short ceremony, we blessed the skulls and Lemurian crystals, with the intent to send healing, activating light energy to the Maya sites, as well as to clear any dark energies or trapped souls.

Circle of Skulls with Rosa central (photo by the author)

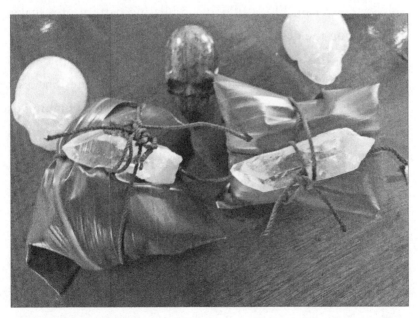

Pair of Rose Quartz/Lapis with Lemurian crystal wrapped in banana leaf ready for placement (photo by the author)

I thought to myself: *This is crazy. Never in my deepest dreams would I have pictured myself activating crystal skulls on a Maya site during a supermoon.*

We then went to a small pyramid with a flat top and lay down, gazing at the moon framed by the trees of the rainforest. Terry noted some dark energies descending towards the pyramid, so we unified our light energies and directed our palms towards the entity, blasting it away from us. We all continued our meditation, feeling into the complex energies of the Maya, then headed off to sleep before our big day of skull placements at Chichén Itzá.

That morning, after breakfast at the hotel, we met our guide for the first part of the day. Since Miguel couldn't join us yet, we hired a gal with great spiritual and archeological knowledge. Walking through the complex, she pointed out how the summer solstice creates on El Castillo an undulating pattern of a snake, representing the descent of the Plumed Serpent Kukulkan to the sacred site. This massive pyramid, 78.7 feet high, has nine levels and is well preserved following excavations and restorations back in the late 1920s. Back in the early '90s I remember climbing its steep steps; today it can't be climbed, due to too many accidents and even a death having occurred when a model tried to ascend it in high heels.

The author with Kukulkan Pyramid in background (photo by Terry Smith)

The guide discussed how the pyramid was built over an underground river (aquifer) and how this river opened up at the north Sacred Cenote and a south Xtoloc Cenote, creating a mouth and tail respectively. It made logical and energetic sense that the Maya would make offerings at the crown and root chakra cenote openings of this snake-like river flowing below the pyramid. Two additional, lesser-known cenotes are also in this area, making a total of four. How they were able to localize the underground river without ground ultrasound and build this immense, heavy pyramid, while perfectly aligning it for solstice, is beyond comprehension to archeologists and scientists.

After our tour of the pyramids, ballcourt, and observatory we headed to the north cenote to place the pair of crystal skulls. Passing vendors selling everything from jaguar masks and pyramids to whistles, we arrived at the edge of the north cenote.

North (Sacred) Cenote (photo by the author)

Setting an intention to heal and send light to this site, we held the skulls to our heart, sending love, then to our Third Eye as we connected them to the oneness of the universe. Holding the powerful bundle wrapped in a banana leaf, with an underhand throw, I released it, watching it arc and land centrally in the cenote's deep green water. As a visible palpable ripple of energy moved across the surface, I envisioned seeing the bundle drift to the floor of the cenote, to clear any dark energies that remained.

We returned back towards the pyramid, depositing Lemurian crystals where we were called to, along with a pair of skulls we placed in an alcove of an overgrown ruin near the south cenote. Seeing a cave near the south cenote, we entered cautiously, wary of snakes, and decided to make a medicine wheel in the sandy floor. Smudging the floor and ourselves with sage, we oriented the selenite and Lemurian crystals in the four directions, then buried them to honor this sacred place.

Reaching into my pack, I grabbed a third pair of crystal skulls wrapped in the leaf. Again, we set intentions, and with a more difficult throw they landed in the south cenote's pool of water—after bouncing off a tree in this heavily forested area. Returning to the main complex and the pyramid, we all felt a sense of bliss and connectedness to the area, hoping that our work would make a difference in further restoring the vibrational light energy of the ancient Maya and Gaia. Sleeping well that night, we woke early to make the long drive west to Uxmal and the Pyramid of the Magician.

Pyramid of the Magician at Uxmal (photo by the author)

Meeting us at the entrance, Miguel informed us how—compared to other Maya sites—the energies differ here. Chichén Itzá was a place of science, technology, and even the training of warriors, but here at Uxmal, the focus was the arts, education, and the divine feminine. "Notice the rounded curvature on this pyramid, contrasted with Chichén Itzá," he said.

The author with Miguel under an Uxmal Ceiba tree (photo by Terry Smith)

"You will see how this site aligns more with feminine energies as we tour it today. I will show you a structure that is believed to have been a library here. And up on the hill over there, some of the most beautiful carved, artistic stonework." We sat down at a sacred Maya Ceiba tree not far from the pyramid and chatted with him in the shade.

As I felt into the field of energies and mysteries of the Pyramid of the Magician I asked Miguel: *This may sound crazy, but I am sensing a large ball of energy deep within this pyramid and a portal near the altar at the top. Is there anything to this insight I'm getting?* Miguel, paused and looked at me with a big smile. "Yes, Fred, I too have sensed the big sphere (ball) of energy inside this pyramid, and it's curious that you mention a portal. Several years ago a French couple attended the evening laser-light show in the nunnery complex behind this pyramid. When it was done, they walked down to the base of the pyramid, and her husband decided to climb up to the off-limits ceremonial platform (altar) on top. Waiting for him patiently, she assumed he would quickly come back out and climb down. Thirty minutes passed and he did not reappear. Worried, she alerted the guards and apologized for him going up without permission. They searched the platform and entire pyramid area, followed by the grounds, for an entire week. He could not be found anywhere. Even the small wells were inspected to see if he'd fallen in. Nothing. Myself and a group of shamans were called to the area for insights. In meditation we concurred that he traveled through the portal on the platform and would hopefully return safely in several years. So in answer to your question, yes, there is a portal, and if you time it right, it's goodbye to this reality." *Wow,* I thought. *Sure hope he's able to walk back into our reality soon for his wife and family.* "Don't think I'll be making a covert operation to climb up there myself," I told Miguel!

We explored the rest of the site, appreciating the amazing carved-stone reliefs at the House of the Turtles and Governor.

House of the Governors, Uxmal (photo by the author)

Following our amazing tour and shared insights from Miguel, Terry and I placed a few Lemurian crystals in cracks amongst the pyramids, and a pair of crystal skulls in a small protected alcove. Blessing this powerful site, our group traveled to sample some Maya honey from a beekeeper down the road. The honey had the richest fruity taste I'd ever sampled, and the beekeeper offered to fill up our empty plastic water bottles with it. The beehive was in a hollowed-out horizontally elevated log, which had a cork at the bottom that he simply pulled out to allow the liquid gold to flow into my bottle. Holes in the top of the log allowed the bees access and the ends were capped. Wow, such a simple and noninvasive way to get honey. So much better than the boxes in the States. Later we visited a shop making perfect ceramic replicas of incense burners, pots, and other artwork. I purchased a beautiful copal incense burner to use in meditation ceremonies for the future.

Replica of traditional Maya incense burner (photo by the author)

Thanking Miguel for his deep spiritual insights and sacred tour of Uxmal, our group drove south towards Tulum, stopping in the ruins of Coba along the way. Renting bikes we pedaled around this expansive beautiful site, stopping at the tall Nohoch Mul Pyramid to make the steep climb up the 120 steps. Breathing light into a large Lemurian and holding it to my heart, I left it in a crack inside the covered platform. Descending back down, we biked over to a smaller pyramid, which had been minimally excavated. Following the narrow trail to the top, I could see out over the canopy of trees. Feeling into this magical pyramid, I decided to leave the last pair of crystal skulls under the roots of trees growing from its summit. Having placed the last pair of skulls, I felt relief and a rise in the energy field around me. Descending slowly, feeling the energy of this pyramid, I made the ride back to the entrance. Being dehydrated, we hopped into a shop to drink another liter of water and made our way to Tulum.

The following day we toured Tulum. The ruins here are more modest, but the turquoise ocean backdrop, palms, and sandy cove beaches make it idyllic.

Tulum, El Castillo (photo by the author)

Tulum, Templo del Dios del Viento/Temple of the Wind God
(photo by the author)

This has become a very popular place to stay, with numerous new lodges just down the beach west of the archeological site. The lodging in this area is more boutique and rustic, with beach bungalows, and caters more to those seeking yoga retreats on the beach than slamming down Margaritas in the more commercial high rises of Playa del Carmen and Cancún to the east.

I remembered how twenty-five years ago, I'd simply parked on the side of the road in a convertible VW bug and walked less than fifty yards to the main temple. Park rangers were there to protect the site, but no gate, and an unimpeded walk up to see it. Things have changed so much now with huge parking lots a half mile away, entrance fees, and the entire area walled off. Not letting it bother me, I recognized the challenges of high volumes of visitors, as we waited in a long line to purchase tickets. It did, however, make me appreciate the more remote and uncrowded sites of Uxmal, Palenque, and others.

After making our final placements in Tulum and spending some time on the beach, I said goodbye to the others and was off to the Cancún airport to fly home. What a meaningful, deep journey to the Yucatán it had been! Miguel had shared a Maya wisdom phrase that stuck with me: In Lak'ech, Ala K'in—which means "I am you, you are me, we are one." The Maya embraced this; after our work here I felt this field of oneness. I could only hope that our work here and in the world at large will help others embrace it as well.

Chapter 7:

The Rapa Nui Vision

A year had passed since my travels to Peru and I continued to make crystal placements and medicine wheels in powerful locations at Sedona and Mount Shasta. These helped to further link the energies of North America (Turtle Island) to South America (Heart Island). Visiting—and making placements at—Angkor Wat, Hawaii, Fiji, Galapagos, Mount Kilimanjaro, and so many other locations expanded and amplified the field of the growing Lemurian grid. I am grateful to friends who were willing to take and place some of my Lemurian crystals in Jerusalem, Teotihuacan, and other sacred areas around the world. I was at a point where, again, I felt my work was done.

Feeling called to attend a plant-medicine ceremony with my friends in Boulder, I showed up with no expectations other than to be in flow with the group. The ceremony began with some gentle yoga, followed by playing the crystal healing bowls. Our group of fifteen or so set intentions, then took a psilocybin-containing (psychedelic) chocolate to help us spirit travel and meditate deeply. Relaxing on my yoga mat, meditating to mantra music playing in the room, I began to feel myself slowly and lightly drifting into the multiverse. The multiverse is that space where I feel and see dimensions beyond our 3-D consciousness, which in a deeper state can extend into the cosmos. I felt the need to move energy in my body, so I walked around a bit, did a few yoga poses, and went into a room where a friend, Maria, was meditating. I asked if I could join her, and after she agreed, I sat on the couch across from her to drop in more deeply.

Moai at Rano Raraku (photo by the author)

Before long, I found myself on another out-of-body spirit trip—again flying south over Central and South America. Within a few minutes I was hovering over a triangular-shaped island off South America, then saw myself flying down into a large volcanic crater and simply placing a large crystal at its base. Wondering where in the world I'd landed, I suddenly had the word *Rapa Nui* come in. I meditated on the island for a good hour, and then opened my eyes to still see Maria sitting there. I asked her, *Have you ever heard of Rapa Nui?* "No," she said. *Neither have I. This sounds out there, but I just spirit traveled to an island and placed a large crystal there.* "Let's look up the name," she suggested.

Finding my phone in the other room, I googled and discovered that Rapa Nui is the native name for Easter Island. *OMG, I've always wanted to go there to see the Moais [carved human figures] and experience the island. I wonder if the island has volcanoes and is triangular-shaped, as I visualized in the journey.* I went to Google Maps, then a satellite view, and was absolutely stunned. Not only was it triangular shaped, but I could see the exact volcanic crater I'd placed the crystal in. Maria smiled at me, and I just sat there, head spinning. *Well, I guess that's where I'm going next.* Telling the story to family the following week, I got another look of disbelief, and resistance to the idea of me making another remote crazy trip. Regardless, I remained committed and began to work on logistics. Time would help me figure this out and manifest this placement.

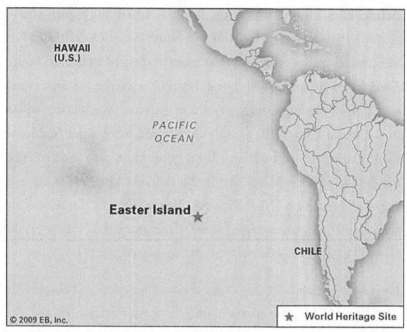

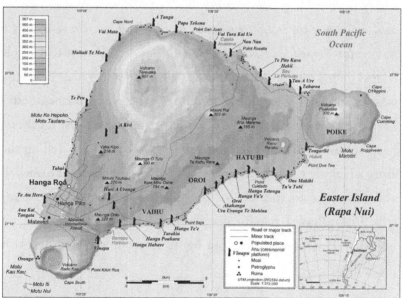

Rapa Nui location in Pacific, https://www.britannica.com/place/Easter-Island; **and Island map showing triangular shape,** https://commons.wikimedia.org/wiki/File:Easter_Island_map-en.svg

Meditating on Rapa Nui, I felt its deep, ancient connection to Lemuria, the mythical lost continent that had sunk deep into the Pacific, according to many who channel on it. Lemuria is thought to predate Atlantis and to have maintained a field of resonate energy that was devoid of darkness (see, for example, descriptions from the much-admired "sleeping prophet," sometimes called "the father of holistic medicine," Edgar Cayce). According to him and others, remnants of Lemuria remain, including the Hawaiian Islands, Rapa Nui, and even Point Reyes, California.[20] Atlantis is thought to have been destroyed by outer forces as a result of the inappropriate use of technology that led it down a path of darkness. While it is difficult to prove or disprove these theories, I felt there was a reasonable amount of cultural storytelling, and channeled information to be open-minded and research further. For example, modern-day archeologists majorly underestimated the size of the Maya territories. The newer technology of LIDAR scanning detected these undiscovered sites and is rewriting history today, doubling the estimated size of their civilization.

I decided to reach out to the Hawaiian Priestess spiritual intuitive/ healer Kahuna Kalei, whom Lee Carroll, the famous channeler of "Kryon," identified as "a pure Lemurian, and one who has awakened to the core seed."[21] I'd done a short ceremony and channeling with her in the last couple years at Waipi'o Valley (Big Island of Hawaii). I knew she was of Lemurian lineage, and she had channeled that in me as well. We had blessed a Lemurian crystal together and placed it on the bluff overlooking the valley that day. If anyone could help me find a shaman at Rapa Nui (Easter Island), it would be her.

Kahuna Kalei (photo provided by her)

Besides, I didn't want to just show up and leave a crystal. Tapping into the energies of this sacred place, I felt the honoring needed to include guidance from the natives in the complex, but isolated Lemurian island. Kahuna was able to connect me with a travel agent who had worked with the shaman on Rapa Nui, and then he reached out to him to work on logistics.

I decided to use the same powerful sacred geometric form of the Unity Grid (Metaforms) with a crystal for this location too. I could sense a need to link Lake Titicaca to Rapa Nui and across to Southeast Asia at Angkor, so I researched if such a line might preexist and was excited to find that a ley line was perhaps re-discovered by Graham Hancock, an author of multiple popular books, "who describes himself as an unconventional thinker who raises controversial questions about humanity's past."[22] The ley line in question, he said, traverses the Great Pyramid, Machu Picchu, and Easter Island and extends to Angkor Wat.[23]

Amazing, I thought. I'd been working an existing ley line without knowing it. Making a placement at Easter Island would connect to placements I'd made at Machu Picchu and Angkor Wat, leaving me only the Great Pyramid to revisit sometime in the near future. I had been to Egypt in 1996, but was not doing my work with crystals back then.

Touring the Museo Antropologico P. Sebastian Englert just outside of Hanga Roa, I came upon a historical map that shows the alignments between Rapa Nui, New Zealand, and the Hawaiian islands. Many of the Polynesian cultures originated within this Pacific/Polynesian triangle; oftentimes they created their own Polynesian subcultures and languages in migrating to remote locations such as Rapa Nui by outrigger sailing canoes. While I have not yet found a discussion of energetic ley lines created by this triangle, I sense that one exists. Standing there, analyzing the thousand or more islands within the triangle, I recalled that I had placed a large Lemurian crystal in sacred Lake Rotorua, on the North Island of New Zealand, eleven months prior and have placed numerous crystals on the Big Island of Hawaii over the last decade. *So cool*, I thought. *I've now placed crystals on the three points of the Polynesian Triangle. Perhaps that will create an additional field of healing resonance within this triangle.*

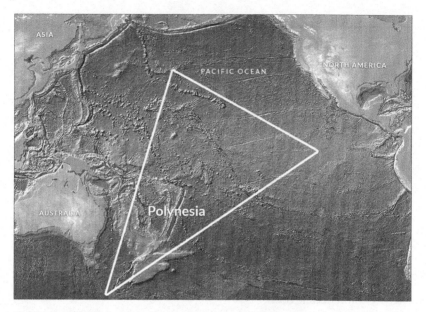

Polynesian Triangle, New Zealand, Hawaii, and Rapa Nui, source: https://divediscover.whoi.edu/history-of-oceanography/polynesian-seafarers/

As the pieces came together I reached out to friends, including Terry, to join me. Finding the flight from Santiago to Easter Island was a big challenge, due to its rising popularity of over a hundred thousand visitors a year. I think we can again thank social media for that.

A little bit of Rapa Nui history: Originally settled by Polynesians between 300 and 700 AD, it was discovered by the Dutch in 1722 on Easter Sunday; hence, the name. It was then visited by the British (including Captain Cook), Spanish, French, Russians, Peruvians, and others in the late 1700s to 1800s and was eventually annexed by Chile in 1837. It was leased out by Chileans to British sheep farmers, further damaging the already-stressed land as well as the archeological sites, as sheep and horses walked on or around them.

Our group arrived in January 2019, flying in on a comfortable 787 Dreamliner, landing on a short, bumpy but paved airstrip next to the small capital of Hanga Roa. Proceeding to the mostly thatched-roof terminal, we grabbed our bags and took a van to a remote ecolodge, with a vast view of the Pacific and pineapple fields below us. The island has only 6,000 locals, so they are a bit overwhelmed by the high volume of tourists. The population is approximately 60 percent indigenous Rapa Nui, and 40 percent Chilean immigrants. Early on, we could feel the tension of the local Rapa Nui people against the Chileans as we drove by large Rapa Nui signs protesting a five-star hotel that had been built on their sacred land. This seemed so reminiscent of what happened to Native Americans on our mainland and on the islands of Hawaii.

Cruising around in an old, rusted Mitsubishi van, with Pau the shaman and his relatives translating and assisting as Rapa Nui guides, we bounced over the potholed roads, touring the key Moai sites, including the famous Ahu Tongariki, with fifteen Moai heads on it.

Ahu Tongariki (photo by the author)

Tina, Pau's cousin who served as a guide and translator, pointed at an ancestral chief of hers represented on this ahu (stone platform), making this site much more meaningful. Several tribes were represented by the face of their ancestral chief; these tribes had seemingly competed to have the most impressive ahu. On all ahus except one, the Moai heads look towards the people and tribe, offering protection, rather than out to the sea. There is, however, one Moai (face of a deified ancestor) that looks to the stars.

Moai looking into the stars at Rano Raraku (photo by the author)

Leaving some crystals in the surrounding area, but not on the ahu, we traveled to the quarry nearby at the volcanic crater Rano Raraku; we were shown how the Moai were cut from the volcanic stone, then "walked" using ropes, sometimes miles, to their final destination on the ahu (platform). At this site there is a unique Moai that looks to the stars, and another that has ships engraved into it, likely representing the Spanish or British ships that visited.

Unfortunately, you can see a few Moai fallen and left in place face down in the quarry region. If they fell, they lost their power and were not taken to the ahu. Also sadly, most of the Moai on the platforms were toppled by warring tribes during civil war and a period of starvation. Collective efforts of the Japanese, UNESCO, and other archeological groups have helped lift many of the fallen Moai back to their original position.

Toppled Moai (photo by the author)

After a long day, we went into town for some amazing local fish. Walking around Hanga Roa, I sited a gelato stand and couldn't resist. I was feeling pretty hot, so I more less inhaled it. Bad idea, as I suddenly felt my heart go into an irregular beat. *Oh, crap*, I thought. *I just put myself in atrial fibrillation! This has happened before when I've chugged ice cold drinks and I should have known better. Oh, man, I don't think I'll be able to get myself shocked out of this on a remote island 2,300 miles from a major medical center. I'll just take some aspirin and hope I flip out of it.* Throughout the night my heart palpitations continued jolting me awake periodically. I remained concerned that I wouldn't flip back into a normal rhythm. I didn't share this with our guides, as I didn't want them to worry about me.

Motu Nui (Birdman Island) from Orongo village overlook with Pau, Rapa Nui shaman, and author (photo by Terry Smith)

The next morning we met with Pau the shaman and our guides to tour the sacred site of Orongo, a village on the rim of the Rano

Kau volcanic caldera, where I had had my vision of placing a crystal in the crater. Here, is also where the infamous local Rapa Nui Birdman competition occurred.

Each tribe would have a competitor who, after scaling down the treacherous cliff, swam across rough, shark-infested water to a small island inhabited by terns. Each would retrieve an egg, secure it with a woven headband, then swim back, scale the cliff, and cross the finish line back at Orongo. For a year the winner would basically be a demigod honored by all, bestowing great honor to his tribe as well. The successful master received the title "Tangata manu" (Birdman), and on presentation of the egg, was escorted to Mataveri, where a great feast was held in his honor; he would live in seclusion for a year in a house at Rano Raraku (the location of the quarry).

We saw the area where the small Moai had been taken by the British; with contention from locals, it continues to reside in the British Museum. They are negotiating its return, for it provides mana (spiritual energy) for Orongo and the entire island. Following this tour, with my heart still beating irregularly, Pau offered to take us to a healing rock on the opposite rim of the volcano. He said that for hundreds of years, his people used it to help cure various ailments. Looking across the beautiful crater lake below, I was excited to make a trip over to this area, which is only accessible with local permission.

We drove the van around to the other side and up a rough dirt road to a small trail. Hiking for a good thirty minutes, we paused periodically to pay respect to a small carved Moai. Feeling more winded than usual, since my heart rate was so irregular, I continued to climb on—excited to reach the crater rim and to feel the energy of the large, magnetic granite-like rock. Pau began to chant a Rapa Nui prayer, perhaps from the hieroglyphic rong-orongo his cousin mentioned he had memorized. Tapping on a large horse jawbone, with the teeth rattling in the sockets, he created a rhythm that was mesmerizing. Of course, I had no idea what the translation was; his cousin said they were healing prayers. I listened and relaxed on the rock. As he continued to recite, suddenly I noticed my heart was beating normally again! Thinking to myself, *Amazing, I didn't come up here with any expectations, but within ten minutes of sitting on this sacred rock I am back into a normal heart rhythm,* I smiled while sitting on the rock and simply said to them, *Wow, thank you. I feel so good being up here on this healing rock.*

I had brought the Unity Grid with crystals in it up to this location on the rim, being worried I wouldn't be able to place it deep in the crater below. Maybe I could leave it here. I even contemplated launching it off the crater rim, but didn't like the idea of it getting banged up on the descent. I'd seen signs and details on the map that only local Rapa Nui can go down to the sacred crater lake. My greatest desire, however, was to fulfill the vision and place it somewhere in the base of the crater, or even in the lake. Anticipating a *no* answer, I said, *Pau, I had a vision that I should place this sphere with a crystal in the crater below to honor this island, your people, help improve its mana, and help heal the world. Would you or another local be willing to place it down there for me?*

He looked me in the eyes and without hesitation said, "Fred, you will go down and place this sphere. You have my permission and I will get permission for you and my relatives to descend early tomorrow morning. I am not in physical shape to make it with you myself, but again, I want you to fulfill this vision" (Tina translating). Hearing him say these words, I almost rolled off the cliff. *OMG, my heart arrhythmia has resolved, and now he's opening the gate for us to descend and make a placement into this sacred crater. I* couldn't believe what I was hearing!

Returning to the ecolodge that night, I felt a magical flow of energy. Once I finally calmed down, I slipped into dream space and awoke, prepared for this spiritual adventure. We arrived early morning at the trailhead and began the 700-foot descent. It had rained the prior night, so the volcanic mud was slippery on the descent. As I looked down at the crater lake, it seemed surreal that this vision was about to be manifested.

Rano Kau crater lake (photo by the author)

Sliding onto my butt a few times, I laughed as I bounced down some sections of the steep trail. Getting closer to the crater base, we were surrounded by lush vegetation that thrives as it wicks the water from the freshwater lake at its base. Looking around in the woods, we found a log to sit on and a nice place to relax and hold our group circle. Each of us passed the sphere, placing our intent into it, holding it to our hearts and our crown chakra. As a group we decided it would be most powerful to place it in the lake to connect to the entire energy field of the crater. Tina shared the local Rapa Nui legend that there is a large blue crystal deep in the crater lake. She was excited that another one would be joining it soon.

About a third of the lake is covered with a thick layer of floating reeds, which allows one to hike on this spongy floating carpet closer to the center. What is most intriguing is this species of reed is also found on the floating islands of Uros on Lake Titicaca! One has to wonder if the Pre-Incas or Incas traveled to Rapa Nui long ago and introduced this species of reed.

Tina asked if I wanted to be the one to swim out and place the sphere. I contemplated it for a while, but then spirit guided me that her royal Rapa Nui lineage made her the perfect one to release this into the sacred crater lake. Having come prepared, she went deeper into the woods—returning with her swimsuit on to accept the challenge. While I thought she might simply jump in naked, I recognized that with her son and relatives there, it was more appropriate to be suited up. She was truly afraid of entering the waters and shared stories of sea monsters and even alien spaceships emerging from the depths. She had pointed out one of these sea monsters in an ancient petroglyph carved on the rock just a hundred feet away from us; she even showed us triangular shapes on the reed mats, which she said were related to space-ships, thinking of them much like crop circles.

We walked out slowly a good fifty yards, over the floating reed mat, until we came to a large opening of water not too far from the center of the lake. As at Lake Titicaca, you could look off the edge of the reed mat and see into the depths below.

Holding the sphere close to my heart, sending pure love to it to spread to the lake and volcano, I released it to Tina, who sat wait-ing on the reed ledge.

Author holding the Unity Grid with enclosed crystals (photo by Terry Smith)

Swimming out gracefully a good thirty feet, she dropped the sphere, allowing it to gently sink to the crater floor below. Swimming back, we smiled, congratulating her for making it back safely. We could all sense a flow of energy following the placement as we walked back towards the trail.

Climbing back up and out of the crater, I looked back into its deep blue waters. I felt such immense gratitude to the universe for once again creating the flow to manifest this shamanic vision. Thanking Tina and her relatives, we made the descent down to Hanga Roa, and celebrated over lunch, enjoying ceviche (seafood cocktail) and other local foods. As I took in the views of waves splashing and foaming against the black lava rocks below our open-air patio, the moment again felt surreal.

The following morning we decided it would be perfect for the group to climb to the highest point on the island after being at the lowest elevation, in the crater of Rano Kau. The tallest volcano is Terevaka, at 1,663 feet; the trailhead begins at Ahu Akivi and is the only platform where the Moai look out towards the ocean. It's a beautiful place to start a hike, viewing the seven Moai heads looking out over the dark blue Pacific Ocean.

Ahu Akivi (photo by the author)

Following a four-wheel-drive trail, we eventually transitioned to a single-track trail and could see the town of Hanga Roa below. The lower slopes have small farms growing plots of vegetables, and as we ascended we were on a short grass-covered volcanic ridge. Looks somewhat like the grassy hills of Scotland. Within a couple hours we reached the summit of Terevaka and took in the panoramic views of the entire island. Small groups of various nationalities arrived, snapping a quick summit shot, then headed back down.

To escape noisy tourists, we continued walking a bit and found a small flat area just below the summit for a light lunch. Feeling into the energies of this volcanic mountain, we decided on a location to make a small medicine wheel. We could feel a higher vibration in this area, which some might call a vortex. Using sage and Palo Santo, we smudged the ground, then dug narrow grooves in the volcanic sand to plant our medicine wheel. Using my compass, we oriented the spokes of selenite and Lemurian, then chanted the Peruvian directions of Pachamama, Mama Killa, Viracocha, Inti, and K'uychi to activate the wheel, as I traditionally do; then used my small rattle to connect the upper, middle, and lower worlds to the wheel.

Medicine Wheel on Mount Terevaka summit (photo by the author)

Looking across the island to the Rano Kau crater, we sent our intentions to align this wheel to the crystal-filled Unity Grid in the crater lake and then to radiate out to all the Lemurian crystals in the grid around the world. The energy from this peak began to feel like a beacon of light shining and connecting to the other points in Peru, New Zealand, Hawaii, Angkor Wat, and beyond.

After burying the crystal medicine wheel, we shouldered our packs and began the two-hour descent. My energy body felt light and interdimensional as I descended. It was our last major placement prior to departure the next day, so we returned to our lodge to do a plant-medicine ceremony to tap into the impact of the crystals we placed. As the psychedelic plant medicine began to take effect, I lay down, eyes closed, in the dark room and began to see iridescent colors and complex 5-D geometry. Mantra music played, and a cool ocean breeze came in through the open windows. Soon I was seeing beams of rainbow light emerging from the depths of Rano Kau crater, and more beams radiating from the summit of Tereveka. I simply observed the radiant light for at least an hour and then saw it connecting to a faraway peak somewhere in the Himalayas. Now, this is wild. Why would I be seeing this rather than something closer, in the Pacific? As I continued to follow this flow of light, the name of the peak came to me: Mount Kailash, the sacred Tibetan peak and place of pilgrimage for Hindus, Buddhist, Jains, and Bonpa ("the Bons"). To Buddhists it is known as Mount Meru.

Mount Kailash (photo by Terry Smith)

Interestingly, Cambodia's Angkor Wat temple represents Mount Kailash, with the central lotus tower and the four corner lotus towers representing the sister peaks.

Angkor Wat (photo by the author)

Pilgrims typically walk in a clockwise direction around this 21,000-foot peak to receive good fortune. Later I learned that "Mount Kailash" is derived from the Sanskrit word *kailas*, which means "crystal" (see definition in citation). "Kailash, kailas, also refers to the ability of the yogi to develop [the] crystalline clarity of their true nature."[24] Wow, how perfect; it made wild sense that the crystals on Rapa Nui would connect to a crystalline peak 12,000 miles away, in the Himalayas of Tibet!

Suddenly I was visualizing what appeared to be a portal in the sky above Kailash, spinning and connected to the cosmos, but also sending strands of energy towards Rapa Nui. Wow, I never would have expected something like this coming in!! Soon, as more energy flowed across the Pacific, I visualized a smaller portal opening up over Rapa Nui. My sense in this deep journey was, Mount

Kailash was sending information or energy to help reactivate an ancient portal over this island. As the portal came back online, more light energy from the cosmos poured in, allowing it to share it out from the island to regions of imbalance around the world. Not only did I see light flowing from the mountain, but I was shown how the melting snows flowed this sacred water into the tributaries of the sacred Ganges River, emptying into the Bay of Bengal, followed by some of this water circulating through ocean currents all the way to Rapa Nui.

Later the next morning I integrated these unexpected visions with the group. Terry had seen spaceships hovering over the island in her visions and reminded me that just six months ago at the base of Kailash in the sacred Lake Manasarovar, she placed a crystal I'd given her.

Perhaps her placement of the one crystal, connecting to this crystalline-like granite pyramid-shaped mountain, was all it took to reconnect through the crystals placed on Rapa Nui.

The five-hour flight back to Santiago, followed by the twelve-hour flight to Denver, gave me plenty of opportunity to contemplate our stay at Rapa Nui. I am forever grateful to my new Rapa Nui friends Pau, Tina, and family for showing me the magical energies of their island and am hopeful that our work there will amplify the mana of their people and the island, allowing this sacred place to help rebalance Gaia, its inhabitants, and the higher dimensions embedded within it.

Chapter 8:

Connecting and radiating the grid around Gaia and into the cosmos

R apa Nui feels like a turning point, but I anticipate lots more work ahead. My role as a physician healer continues, but I see it expanding into the realm of helping others awaken. Whether this is by sharing spiritual insights through my monthly speaking engagements or perhaps leading retreats, time will tell. My speaking engagements are not for money or recognition. Rather, I see them as an honor—to help others improve their mind, body, and spiritual balance. It's my dharma.

Continuing this wild, unusual calling of placing crystals to create grids, activations, and ley lines extends beyond my three-dimensional role on this planet and I will continue to flow with it. I've made so many placements that I can't remember to log them all on the map. Honoring local sacred spots, such as Sedona, Shasta, and the Redwoods, and international sites in Southeast Asia, the Greek islands, and even the summit of Mount Kilimanjaro continues to beg a few questions:

- What is the purpose of doing this work?

- Will it make a difference?

- Is there an end point?

Sometimes I feel it's not the placement of crystals that matters, but the heart openness and compassion it generates as I place them to honor Gaia. Perhaps there is a growing coherent field of energy developing from the placement of crystals too. While some may call me pagan, they are wrong. It is beyond what can be defined or labeled in our simple human categoric manner.

We now know from recent scientific studies that we can shift our own DNA through mindfulness-based practices, especially when we resonate it with love, gratitude, forgiveness, and compassion. I detailed this in my book *Spiritual Genomics*. We also know we can reduce pain and inflammation through the placement of acupuncture needles on the human body. Furthermore, human touch and energy work can aid in healing.

Is it possible that we can shift the energetic properties of Gaia, creating grids and ley lines, by—with loving intention—placing crystals, stones, and temples, or by other means? My intuition says yes. While we are continuing to mine and pollute the Earth with our growing populations, we must do our best to reciprocate what we have taken from her by protecting her waters, forests, and life-forms. As we seek a planetary yin/yang, or Masculine/Feminine, balance, a shift towards protecting Earth will occur. Currently we are in a masculine (yang) cycle, trending with resistance into a more balanced yin/yang realm. As this pot is being stirred locally and globally, individuals will continue to step up to the plate and move this trend forward. Many of us will be ridiculed in disrespectful, thoughtless ways by those who seek more power and material assets. We must stand strong and united to overcome this darkness. In doing so, we must disrupt the darkness, fill it with light, and awaken many more to help save ourselves and the planet.

What can we do individually and as a society here in the States and, as much as possible, globally?

- Stand up for more environmental protection of our lands and oceans

- Drastically reduce air and water pollution (including the use of pesticides)

- Reduce and mitigate EMF and other harmful frequencies (i.e., 5G wireless)

- Reduce carbon fuel consumption/emissions and promote sustainable, clean, green energy solutions.

- Seek peaceful solutions to interpersonal conflicts and, on a bigger scale, avoid wars.

- Love each other authentically, and seek a deep, sacred, sexual union with our partner's.

- Allocate resources to prevent world hunger and disease

- Elect responsible, ethical, compassionate leaders that embrace sustainable solutions for all on our planet,

- Learn, discover, remember, and rebirth the personal and planetary healing techniques of ancient civilizations

- Again, last but not least, awaken others to the world beyond our materialistic third-dimension—motivating them to help heal one another and the planet we live on. Whether this is by volunteering to provide water filtration to prevent disease in a remote African village, reducing plastics in our oceans, or placing crystals around the world, it all makes a difference.

So, as I make my placements, and encourage others to follow paths of light, as unusual or seemingly random as they may be, I enter into a space of timeless love. My human existence is just a nanosecond on this planetary timeline, but the energetic imprint I leave for the enhancement of life and the health of our planet is infinite. Perhaps 500 million years from now, a life-form, human or not, will pick up one of the hundreds of crystals placed around the world and say, "Wow, how, when, and for what reason was this left here?" My hope is that they will see it as a gift of gratitude and love to Earth and all its inhabitants. To all that is, or could have been, even if we wipe ourselves off the face of this planet, each crystal will share a field of energy infused with love and oneness, and a hope for a better tomorrow for Gaia and all her beings.

In Lak'ech, Ala K'in— "I am you, you are me, we are one."

Acknowledgments

I am thankful for all the support I received from my family and friends while I wrote this book. Thank you especially to my family. My amazing ex-wife Theresa, daughter Brooke, son Keaton, and the family dogs for their patience during this writing. Without their help and flexibility, I never would have found the time to complete this. Thank you to my office staff, Austyn Lewis and Laura Paolicelli, for keeping things organized and efficient at work so that I had more time to write.

Gratitude to Margaret A. Harrell for her excellent editorial work and for being willing to do a second book with me. Thank you to Darlene Swanson for her amazing design and formatting work.

Thanks also to my spiritual friends, who have helped me maintain my passion to try to make the world a better place to live in and for understanding my weirdness. These include Terry Smith, Kathy Ohara, Amy Munroe, Jonathan and Andi Goldman, Shelley Genovese, Jyoti Stewart, Gurpreet Gill, Greg and Gail Hoag, Yves Nager, Eunjung Choi, Kahuna Kalei, Pau, Tina Walters, Marco Aristondo, James Loan, don Oscar Miro Quesada, Jonette Crowley, Daniel Gutierrez, and Miguel Angel Vergara. Thanks to many others who have helped me along the way, and to the future light and energy healers I hope to meet who will assist in accelerating the clearing of darkness on our planet.

Last but not least, thanks to Gaia for nurturing and supporting life, and to the goddesses, gods, and unseen forces of the cosmos that help maintain life and structure in our seemingly infinite universe surrounding us.

Endnotes

1 "5D optical data storage," Wikipedia, https://en.wikipedia.org/wiki/5D_optical_data_storage.

2 "Peru for Less: Intihuatana," https://www.machupicchu.org/ruins/intihuatana.htm.

3 "Machu Picchu: What is the Intihuatana stone?" https://www.explorandes.com/machu-picchu-intihuatana-stone/.

4 See Liza Prado and Gary Chandler, the section "Temples XII and XIII" in *Moon Yucatán Peninsula*, for additional information; online at https://books.google.com/books?id=30HXCwAAQBAJ&pg=PT865 &lpg=PT865&dq=Temple+XII+(Moon)+and+XIII,+adjacent+to+t he+Temple+of+Inscriptions.&source=bl&ots=HqYaYP2gkp&sig=A CfU3U0vnN3CWrk08ipbgM7owKp7M29m-g&hl=en&sa=X&ved= 2ahUKEwjYhNzIzvvlAhVPnlkKHYFlAuQQ6AEwE3oECA0QAQ#v =onepage&q=Temple%20XII%20(Moon)%20and%20XIII%2C%20 adjacent%20to%20the%20Temple%20of%20Inscriptions.&f=false.

5 Under the entry "K'inich Janaab Pakal."

6 Christopher Minster, "The Sarcophagus of Pakal," Jan. 15, 2018, https://www.thoughtco.com/the-sarcophagus-of-pakal-2136165.

7 Mark Cartwright, "Palenque," Oct. 17, 2014, https://www.ancient.eu/Palenque/.

8 Tom Clynes, https://www.nationalgeographic.com/news/2018/02/maya-laser-lidar-guatemala-pacunam/.

9 "Chaco Canyon: Observation: The Great Houses," https://www.exploratorium.edu/chaco/HTML/time2.html.

10 "Solar Astronomy in the Prehistoric Southwest," http://www.hao.ucar.edu/education/archeoslides/slide_20.php. "The remnant of this supernova [SN-1054], which consists of debris ejected during the explosion, is known as the Crab Nebula and is located in the constellation Taurus.

(See "Supernova Pictograph," https://www2.hao.ucar.edu/Education/SolarAstronomy/supernova-pictograph.)

11 "Chaco Research Archive," http://www.chacoarchive.org/cra/chaco-sites/casa-rinconada/.

12 I.Connect website, http://iconnect2all.com/products/pleiadian-communication-portal/.

13 "Quetzalcoatl," https://en.wikipedia.org/wiki/Quetzalcoatl.

14 John Taylor (1892) [1882], *An Examination into and an Elucidation of the Great Principle of the Mediation and Atonement of Our Lord and Savior Jesus Christ.*

15 "Pre-Hispanic City of Chichen-Itza," https://whc.unesco.org/en/list/483/.

16 "The Mitchell-Hedges Crystal Skull: Laboratory Tests," and "The Mitchell-Hedges Crystal Skull," https://www.crystalskulls.com/mitchell-hedges-crystal-skull.html.

17 Mysteries: Ancient Mysteries—Crystal Skulls," https://www.mysterypile.com/crystal-skulls.php.

18 "The Lodge at Chichen Itza," https://www.mayaland.com/the-lodge-at-chichen-itza/.

19 "Crystal Skull: Max," https://www.crystalskulls.com/max-crystal-skull.html.

20 See https://www.crystalinks.com/lemuria.html.

21 "About," Kahuna Kalei website, http://www.kaleiiliahi.com/about.html.

22 ""Graham Hancock," Wikipedia, citing his books and website, http://blogs.discovermagazine.com/d-brief/2018/09/27/maya-lidar-scans-60000-new-structures/#.XdHSUzJKjUo.

23 See Jim Alison, "Exploring Geographic and Geometric Relationships along a line of Ancient Sites around the world," May 2001, https://grahamhancock.com/geographic-geometric-relationships-alisonj/.

24 "Kailas," Yogapedia, https://www.yogapedia.com/definition/7558/kailas.

Illustrations

Appendix:

Google Maps
Lemurian Crystal Grid

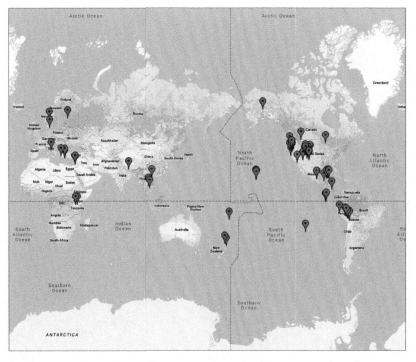

https://www.spiritualgenomics.com/global-map-of-activations

About the Author

Fred Grover Jr., M.D., is the author of *Spiritual Genomics* (2019), which details how you can change your DNA to a healthier, more optimal state through mindfulness and healthy lifestyles. He's a board-certified family physician, entering his twenty-seventh year of clinical practice in Denver. He is an assistant clinical professor of Family Medicine for the University of Colorado, frequently teaching residents in the Integrative Medicine elective, and has researched and published articles on transcranial near-infrared light therapy for treatment of traumatic brain injury. His unique private practice focuses on mind-body health, including two rooms that are dedicated to sound healing and energy work. In addition to providing modern allopathic and regenerative medicine, whenever possible he looks for natural means to address inflammation and disease.

Beyond holistic patient care he is passionate about the health of our planet, supporting many environmental causes, and minimizes his carbon footprint the best he can by powering his home primarily via solar energy. His adventurous spiritual travels often include ceremonies with indigenous shamans, and a major part of these travels also includes honoring Gaia by the placement of crystals described in this book. Following this unusual path with one foot in the 3-D world and the other in the multidimensional, he maintains a heart-centered dharmic flow for the planet, its life-forms, and the surrounding cosmos

Made in the USA
Las Vegas, NV
02 January 2024

83831825R00100